When several ch[obscured] -ties of their variously troubled lives, they discover a most powerful remedy in the form of The Magic Formula, which is delivered by a man who suddenly appears before them.

A MODEL FOR LIVING

"You created the mess that you are in, and it took a lot of time and effort. Is it not reasonable that some time and effort are required to bring about change?" Deliverance asked.

"I suppose so," Steve said reluctantly.

"The magic formula has its own perfect timing, and that is when I will share it with you. If you have a formula that produces results but you have no idea why the formula works or any of the principles involved, then you become dependent either on the formula or on the person who gave it to you. How different is that from any other addiction?"

Inside this book you will find something very important waiting just for you. How you put The Magic Formula to use is up to your needs, strengths and determination. The formula is a profound tool, and you are the magic. Accept the gift, and put it to good use.

ALSO BY MICHAEL J. ROADS

TALKING WITH NATURE

JOURNEY INTO NATURE

JOURNEY INTO ONENESS

INTO A TIMELESS REALM

GETTING THERE

The Magic FORMULA

it works!

by Michael J. Roads

SilverRoads Publishing Cleveland 2003

PUBLISHED BY SILVERROADS PUBLISHING, llc

Published in the United States
by SilverRoads Publishing, llc
3029 Prospect Avenue
Cleveland OH 44115 U.S.A.
216.588.0099
james@silverroads.com

If you are unable to order this book from your local
bookseller, you may order directly from the publisher.
Call 1.866.409.3434 toll free.

LIBRARY OF CONGRESS CONTROL NUMBER: 2003101550

ISBN 0-9729145-1-X

Manufactured in the United States of America
10 9 8 7 6 5 4 3 2
First Edition

To all those men who hurt,
wherever or whoever you are,
this book is dedicated to you.

Know that you can win the struggle
and be the man you want to be.

There always are people to acknowledge with the birth of a new book. Some are the obvious ones, like my beloved wife, Treenie. She continually has encouraged me to explore my feelings and expand my boundaries. My writing stems from this. Thank you, my darling.

The first part of a book that is seen is the cover. The cover is an essential and integrated part of the whole. A book is one whole expression, not the sum of its parts. Seeking the right cover art is rather like looking for a four-leaf clover. They exist, but they are not easy to find. When Chris Dieck appeared from the far flung reaches of close by, I knew that our search had been rewarded. Thank you.

To the Group of Four, I thank you with all my heart for taking this and running with it.

INTRODUCTION

It is usual in today's fiction to state that all the characters in one's book are fictitious, and these characters certainly are. Unfortunately, they have millions of counterparts in every country of the world. In fact, the resemblance to a vast number of men is uncanny. You know men like Gus and Mac, or Steve and Pete, and you may be a Mike. Although this primarily is a book about men, it is not only for men. Just as it may show men a different, more expanded view of the world, so it offers women an expanded insight into men — and life.

I am a man who has struggled and hurt in life, but I could never give up on my search for Self and inner peace. Today, I know who I am: I experience that peace. This book is designed to help those people who are hurting. In Truth, we were never meant to struggle and hurt, never meant to win or lose, or succeed or fail. As human beings, we are on this planet simply to experience life in all its many facets, and by that experience, to grow and expand in our awareness of Self. But — and it's a big but — we have to live. We have to feed and clothe ourselves and provide housing and income for our families.

For so many men — and women — it becomes either one, or the other. We either follow our path of Self-awareness, and pay little attention to the everyday world of success or failure as we struggle along, or we become addicted to the materialism of life, hurting as we get caught by the eternal addiction of always wanting more, particularly when we become emotionally attached. Some of us even manage to combine these two streams of expression, and we struggle and hurt as we are pushed and pulled either one way or the other.

Although I don't really like the word, I am a teacher. My world combines the inner awareness and outer materialism in a flow of easy harmony — and it is easy! One day I listened as a friend shared how, despite doing several of our five-day Roadsway Re***treats, he still found it difficult. He still hurt. We talked, and I said to him, "What you really need is a magic formula. You have the knowledge, but you lack a system to consciously apply it."*

And, because I am a story teller, I wrote this book for him and all the many hundreds of thousands of people like him. This is not a fairy tale. It is a powerful book that teaches you how to find, in your daily life and living, a way to be happy and fulfilled.

CHAPTER ONE

THE GANG OF SIX

It was to be their third reunion, and Mike was on his way to meet the other members of the gang of six. Originally they had come together as kids, all living in the same area, and had formed a deep friendship. Although this friendship was born from the tears and frustrations, the highs and lows of childhood, it contained all the necessary ingredients required to endure the years of growing up. Together they had passed through their troubled teenage years, becoming so close that it seemed impossible to live without having each other in their lives.

They were wrong, of course. In fact, they once had been a gang of seven, almost inseparable, until Ginger got his first motorbike. There was a nasty incident. When the police found Ginger's bloodied body under the truck, it had been headless. Apparently, late one night he had gone at full speed into the rear of a stationary truck. The coroner's verdict probably was as accurate as anything was likely to be. It seems that Ginger definitely had been sober, but inexperienced and probably tired — a deadly combination. Almost certainly, Ginger had thought the truck was moving along at a normal speed in front of him and made his fatal calculations accordingly as he accelerated to overtake.

After that, they were the gang of six. Together, they sat at Ginger's funeral, receiving angry and hostile glares from his parents. Ginger's mother and father never had approved of their son's closeness to the gang, and blamed the boys for leading their son astray. The fact that he was the first of the gang even to have a motorbike passed the parents' attention unnoticed. That, of course, is life. If people get hurt, someone has to be blamed. Innocent as they were, in this case they were the gang of six.

Mike was unable to shrug off Ginger's abrupt death. *Ah well, that's life*, should have worked nicely, but it did not work out that way. He was haunted for months by a feeling of intense vulnerability. His thoughts strayed constantly to this first introduction to death. One moment alive, elated, speeding through the night on a beautiful new bike, then ... splat! And it's all over. Had Ginger felt anything? Mike doubted it. Alive, feeling, enjoying, expressing ... then, nothing. It stuck in Mike's mind for a long time before gradually fading, but by then, Ginger's accident had affected him in many subtle ways. For a start, it prompted him to question life. What is life? Do we have life, or does life have us? If we have life, is it simply a body experience that we lose if we lose the body, or is it something more? If life has us, how can it lose us? Is life inept, incapable of holding on, or is there something more? It was that *something more* that intrigued Mike.

However, many years had passed since then, and their childlike beliefs of being *inseparable* had been fragmented so easily when each of the gang had started dating. Mike often thought how strange it was that girls had come so readily between him and the others. And yet, he realized, they did not really come between us so much as give us an excuse to move apart and do the necessary growing that only time, experience and individuality can supply.

Late one evening, the gang of six, then in their late teens, were sitting in the Matador restaurant. After the food, beer, wine and much raucous laughter, they made a vow that they would all meet in this same place every ten years for the rest of their lives. They all had clasped hands, and with due ceremony, Mike solemnly poured a glass of red wine over their hands, proclaiming this to be the blood of their lives, mixed and mingled, and destined to meet each decade or to horribly die. Despite being rather dramatic, it was meant to be funny, but none of them laughed. They just sat and stared at each other for minutes on end until Lenny said in a soft solemn voice, "So be it." Then, in the same quiet, intense manner, Gus, Steve, Mac and Pete all echoed his words. Mike had said nothing, a bit shocked by what was happening. Lenny looked at him. "How about you, Mike?"

"So be it," Mike said. "But what happens when this place is pulled down? We know we can't always meet here."

They looked at each other, then they all turned to Mike.

"It was your idea," Lenny said.

"Okay. If this place has gone, then we meet at the nearest restaurant to here."

And so it had been.

The gang of six met at the Matador ten years later. Despite the fact that they were scattered and out of touch, they all had turned up at the still functioning Matador. By now they were in their late twenties, and — brash and loud as young men are inclined to be — they dined, wined, drank and chatted their way far into the night. Several of them admitted that they had showed up at the Matador several nights in a row, each not prepared to be the one who was not there. After ten years, they were not sure whether it was a pledge or a curse they had vowed all those years ago, and they were not prepared to risk it.

They had each shared to the group accounts of their own main events of the last ten years, but had they? Mike knew that he did not. He had seriously edited his version. And because of his own deception, he recognized the same type of spaces in the stories of the others as they also shared their adventures. Despite this, it was a wonderful meeting of old friends, and there and then, they renewed their vow to do it again exactly one decade later. Mike had come prepared with a hundred-year wallet calendar, so they each wrote down the exact day and date as it would be in ten years time.

Ten years passed, and they all turned up again.

This time, however, the Matador had been demolished and was part of a huge block of flats, but each man had tracked down the nearest restaurant, The Ocean's Basket, and were there on the given evening. Now in their late thirties, the many differences among them began to show up. It was obvious that Lenny, with all his vast potential, was stuck in life. He told them he was unmarried, in a job that he hated, and living with his widowed mother. He was rapidly going bald and was deeply bothered by it. His once high self-esteem was now low, his facial expression one of anguish and failure.

The story from Gus was almost the opposite. He was successful in his work as a draughtsman and contentedly married with two children. He was short, getting fat, and also balding, and could not care less. For him, life was good.

Steve's life was just so-so. He had gone into the merchant marines and lived a regimented life. He lived a *could be better, could be worse* sort of existence. He was not married and had no woman in his life, yet he obviously longed for one. His self-esteem was low, but covered by a thinly veiled veneer of *everything's okay*.

Mac was an academic. His career was showing great promise, and he expected to be a professor fairly soon. His problem was in his marriage, and although he said little about it, the unsaid spoke volumes. All in all, he skirted life on the edges of depression, indecision and aimless haste.

Pete somehow had a bit of all their problems, but none of it seriously. He was a married police sergeant, big, slow-moving, but quick-witted. He was content with life, going nowhere in particular, and seemed remarkably unconcerned by any of it. He had no children, but not, he told them with a pronounced wink, through lack of trying.

And then there was Mike. He was happily married, with two children, unsure about life, uncertain about himself, but happy enough working in sustainable ecosystems. He, too, had thinning hair, but was unbothered by it. The only certainty in his life was the love he shared with his wife, Tessa. Mike was on what he considered his path — a path of inquiry into the meaning of life, the meaning of self: the why's, how's, where's and when's of it all. This path was shared by Tessa, who had a similar interest in spirituality.

So once again, drawn together by a fading common bond, the gang of six ate and drank their way late into the night, and once more, they renewed their vows to meet again, same place, same time, in another ten years. The same hundred-year wallet calendar provided the day and date, and another half glass of red wine poured over their clasped hands made it all seem very, very real once again.

Another ten years of intense living passed by.

So here they were, ready for the third meeting of the gang of six. Now in their mid- to late-forties, they all were very changed. So uncertain was Mike, he no longer was sure that meeting each decade was such a good idea, but he had traveled a few thousand miles to be here, and this was the evening.

CHAPTER TWO

A TIME TO LET IT LOOSE

As Mike looked at the others in the gang, he felt faintly shocked. This definitely was not a good idea. They should have called it quits last time. My God, Lenny was dead and buried, and he had not known. Gus told him about it. Lenny had suffered a heart attack. Heart attack! Christ, how can a heart attack anyone? If anything in the body was harmless, surely it was the heart. He had never even thought about it before, but now Lenny was dead. And from a heart attack.

Mike sighed, his head in his hands, as he struggled with the reality of his old friend's death.

"Mike, are you okay?" asked Gus.

"Yeah," Mike sighed, "I'm okay. Just a bit shocked about poor Lenny. This bloody heart attack business gets to me. How the hell can a heart attack anyone? It's stupid."

Gus laughed. "It's you being stupid. Heart attack is just words. It really means nothing like it sounds."

"Yeah, tell that to Lenny," Mike said tiredly. "I'm sure that he'll appreciate knowing that it's nothing."

Gazing around the spacious room of the Offbeat Eatery, Mike thought that it should have been named the Deadbeat Eatery when the restaurant had last changed hands. Not that it was a bad place, he thought, but it seemed a downhill move from the former, Ocean's Basket. That had been definitely upmarket. The walls were now papered with a bamboo-type pattern, making it feel immediately casual and relaxed. As he stared hard at the pattern close to their table, he realized that each bamboo cane was an overlaid fabric strip, creating a remarkably authentic effect, adding credibility to the overall appearance. A generous number of people were scattered among the other tables, indicating that the locals considered the food to be good. As he glanced over the patrons, a lone elderly man a few tables away gave him a smile of such intimacy that Mike was startled.

Unable to meet the candid, unreserved eye contact, Mike looked away hastily. Slightly depressed, he listened again to the talk as it drifted around the table where the five friends were seated. Gone was the loud, crass laughter. Instead, they eyed each other with reserve, as though poker players holding their cards tightly against their chests.

Smoke billowed around Gus as he puffed steadily on a fat cigar, while further around the table, Pete inhaled deeply on a menthol cigarette. Mike decided that the combined effect left a lot to be desired, making him feel vaguely nauseous.

"Are you two going to puff that shitty smoke in our faces all evening?" he asked.

"You'll survive," Pete mumbled, downing his beer.

For a long while they just stared at each other, all very aware that they were now a bunch of strangers. Given a new opportunity, none of them would choose to be here.

Mike gave an inner sigh. God, they had nothing in common anymore. Pete, Steve and Gus were all downing quite copious quantities of beer, while he and Mac stayed with wine. Mike preferred a nice Chardonnay, but Mac seemed to have no favourite at all. He simply drank for the sake of drinking, and Mike was not even sure that he tasted it. What a mess, he sighed to himself, as the silence lingered.

Steve broke the tension in a sudden, violent declaration.

"Shit! We sit here full of crap, trying to pretend that everything is rosy. Apart, that is, from Lenny's death. That's one of life's big turds, and we all get it eventually."

"Thanks for that remarkable insight," Mac replied, "but speaking for myself, life could be a lot worse. I'm now acknowledged in my field as an expert, so I really can't grumble."

"And your marriage?" asked Mike.

Suddenly deflated, Mac sighed and shrugged, "What marriage? I don't have one. Betty walked out on me three years ago. But I learned that I can live without her."

"Even a bad woman is better than a good wanking," Steve said philosophically, "and I should know."

Mac colored. "Yeah, well you would. We're not all like you ... thank God."

"Well, thanks for that," Steve sneered, "but that bright red face of yours gives you away, old buddy."

"Hey ... hey." Mike stood up, hands spread out in a gesture of peace. "What in the hell's got into us? I didn't travel thousands of miles to come and fight or to listen to one. We go back a long way, remember. Christ, if we could get through our teenage years without fighting each other, surely, as adults, we can manage now." He looked around, smiling at the others. "I have a suggestion to make. We all have our secrets, let's not crap around about that. But here, with us, that secret's safe. I give you my word that any secret shared here will never pass my lips. So, hey, you know what we can do ... "

Sitting down, Mike put one hand out to the others, and held a half glass of red wine in the other. "Let's hold hands and make a vow of silence that anything spoken here is held sacrosanct, so that we can each unburden ourselves. And a terrible death to he who breaks the vow."

Hesitantly, but one by one, the hands came together, and Mike poured the red wine over them. They looked into each others' eyes anxiously. What they saw must have been reassuring, because, one by one, they relaxed, smiling.

Sitting again, Mike said, "Anyone care to kick off? And don't feel forced. I'll start if no one else wants to."

"What the hell, I can kick this little baby along," Steve muttered, and taking a long drink from his glass, he looked challengingly at the others.

"My life is a first class shit-house. I've managed to stuff-up in just about everything I've ever tried. And believe-you-bloody-me, I have tried. I started off in the merchant marines, as you guys well know, and that quickly proved to suck. I stuck with it for the required time, hoping that somehow it would work out; but it didn't ... and hasn't. Nothing has. It's like I have a bloody jinx. Everything stuffs up. Every relationship, every job, everything. Given time, I'm sure I could stuff up our friendship ... and that's about all I have now that's worth having."

Embarrassed and defiant, he stared at them, one by one. "So, that's my story in a nutshell. How I screwed up doesn't really matter. I just did. In fact, I've reached the place where I really don't know anything else. The fact is, I reckon Lenny is the lucky one. I even tried to top myself once and actually stuffed that up as well."

Mike stared at him, aghast, not caring about the tears that threatened to spring from his eyes. Suddenly, without thought, he was on his feet and around the table, embracing his friend.

"Steve, oh Steve. Oh Christ, if only I could wave a magic wand and change it." Mike hugged him, slowly rocking with the pain he felt for quite some time, before he became embarrassed by his emotional reaction. Finally, not knowing what to say, he returned to his seat.

One by one, the other three got up and embraced Steve. At first they, too, felt some embarrassment; but soon it was just the expression of caring, along with the inner dread that it could so easily have been any one else in the group.

Nobody felt like talking after Steve's confession, so more beer and wine were poured to ease the tension. And it slowly did.

Gus looked around the group and cleared his throat. He had changed physically so much in the last decade that Mike had a problem relating to him as the short, wiry, slim little Gus of their youth. Gus was now totally bald, fat as a barrel, and waddled rather than walked. Mike could not help but think that here was a heart attack candidate if ever there was one. But Gus was alive, energetic, seemingly as full of humor as ever.

"If I was to look at my life and judge it, I could not call myself either a success or a failure," Gus began. "I do know that I love my wife a lot more than she loves me, and that I adore my two girls, Jenny and Mandy. I also know that all of them take me completely for granted, and I sometimes wonder if any of them are even capable of love." Gus's face screwed up in a tight grimace, and he looked away sadly. "I have never even faced those thoughts before this moment, and I had to say them aloud to know that they're true. It's so true that it terrifies me. And do you know what is even more strange? It doesn't matter. So long as I can love them, and they are in my life, I'll settle for that. It's all I have, really."

He took a gulp of beer, and belched. His face was sad, exposed and raw.

"I know they think that I'm a sad, fat, silly little bugger, who should have a stroke or heart attack any time soon, and will then be out of their way." He shook his head pensively. "Life is bloody weird. At work I'm the best draughtsman on the team. I'm respected for my skill. They talk of me as successful, a man to watch ... and at home, where none of my work skills are needed, I'm bugger all."

Mike realized that Gus was no longer being the funny man, and he now knew who hid behind the funny-man image of the past. Mike knew, that like all of them, Gus wore the mask that he wanted others to see. Without his mask, Gus was an unhappy, dejected man.

Gus smiled sadly. "Funny, but it helps having said it. I don't feel quite so alone. Not quite such a fraud. When you daren't even face your deeper thoughts, daren't let them come to the surface, that's a lonely, isolated place to be. And I've been there for a long time now."

He smiled at the others and held up his glass. "So, thanks, guys. Thanks for listening. Steve can now ponder if his life is the worst after all. I know that I would not swap, but only because I'm more comfortable with the devil I do know, rather than one I don't. At least Steve is not bound by bonds of pain the way I am. What I would like to know is simple. Where do I go from here? Is this the rest of my life? Can I change it?" He shook his head in defeat. "I just don't know."

Mike shook his head as well, feeling quite dazed, and raised his glass.

"Here's to our good fortune; may the sun continue to shine on us."

It was a brave attempt at humor that did not work.

Looking rather shaken, nobody even smiled. So Mike had another attempt.

"Anybody else?" he joked. "Now's the time to let it loose. Take your turn for a profound emotional purge."

Glancing around beneath his dense, black, bushy eyebrows, Pete spoke up.

"I reckon I'm as ready as I'm ever going to be. So far all I've heard is problems. I get to hear them every day. I'm a police sergeant, remember. I was a sergeant the last time we met, I'm still a sergeant, and I will be if we meet a decade from now. That's if any of us are still alive by then."

For a big man, his voice was mild and soft. He carried a fair paunch on him, yet moved with a smooth ease. His hair was as black as his eyebrows, standing in a stiff crew-cut.

"You will probably laugh at my problem, and sure enough, it's small next to some of yours, but it's a problem that rules my life. You see, I'm a nice guy, and so long as I stay a nice guy, I'm well-liked. And I like being liked. I like being popular. But I also want promotion. Years ago, I thought that I didn't, but I do. Doreen, my wife, she keeps badgering me to sit for promotional exams, and it's even what I want. But somehow, I just can't."

Mike stared at Pete, a puzzled frown on his face. "What do you mean, you can't? Of course you can."

Pete shook his head sadly. "It ain't that simple. Every one of the men who climbs the ladder of promotion becomes more and more isolated, with fewer friends. The back-stabbing intensifies, while what gets said behind their backs would make your hair curl. Despite all the *yes, sir,* and *very good, sir*, it's a dog-eat-dog life, and that's part and parcel of promotion. Once you move on the promotion track, it's no longer possible to be one of the boys."

"But what about being sergeant?" Steve asked.

"It's okay at sergeant. I can look after the lads, and by being careful, I'm still one of them. We can drink together after hours, laugh and share a joke, and this is something I value. Hell, it's more than that, it's something I need. If an inspector even walks past us in the hotel, the lads all go quiet, waiting until he is out of earshot again. Being as aware of that as I am, I'm not sure that I could live with it. With promotion the camaraderie has gone, dead, kaput."

"Seems to me that you have to make a choice." Gus said, shrugging. "It looks like you can't have it both ways."

"Yeah, I know," Pete replied. "But it's getting to the point of a crisis. I'm damned if I do, and I'm damned if I don't. I don't want to mess things up between me and Doreen, nor between me and the lads, so I'm stuck in a bog of my own stupid inadequacy. And I am inadequate at this point in my life. Oh sure, I can help someone else in their crisis, but I'm unable to solve my own problems. And I don't have long to resolve it. Any time now I could be passed over as too old and too undecided. You know the stuff. The word goes around. Pity about poor old Pete. They passed him by for some new lad. And once that happens, it's the end of the line."

He shrugged heavily. "Ah well, it's really my problem, and it's certainly one of my own making, but I am the way I am."

"Jeeze, and to think I bust my gut to get here just so I could hear all these sad stories," Mike said jokingly.

Mac, who steadily had been drinking his multiple wines, lurched to his feet, stating in a loud voice, "Piss problems, the lot of you. If you want to hear about problems, listen to this."

He swayed, and Mike grabbed his arm, pulling him down into his seat.

"Okay, Mac, so long as this has turned into a real purge, go for it. But keep your voice down a bit."

Mac took a deep breath, bracing himself. "So I'm a bloody professor now. So bloody what. A professor in English bloody literature. So what? Nobody cares. When I was a kid, being a professor was all I could think about. The prestige that I imagined went with it was all a lie. I thought I would be Mister Big." He shook his head wobbly. "But it isn't like that. Nobody cares. It only has prestige to those who know nothing at all, and they don't care either."

He looked at them challengingly from under his eyebrows, his eyes furtive.

"And then there's sex. Nobody's really talked about that, have they? My sex life is completely stuffed, and all I mostly can seem to think about is sex. Sex, sex, sex. My mind is stuffed full of endless fantasies. And none of it is nice, gentle, safe sex."

He glared savagely at Steve. "You think you know what wanking is? Huh! I sometimes wank half a dozen times a day, and it's never enough ... and it's never any bloody good."

His voice dropped to a soft, hesitant whisper. "And I don't know how to stop. I don't know how to get rid of the sexual thoughts that haunt my day, fill my mind and screw up my life. Suicide? No, I've never tried to deliberately top myself, but I've created dangerous situations for myself over and over and come out unscathed every time."

He looked around at the others. "So that's my secret can of worms. It's nasty stuff, and to be honest, I'm ashamed of myself. So what do I do about it, guys? Can you tell me? Can anybody?"

Steve was sitting bolt upright, a look of astonishment on his face. "Shit! If that don't beat all. And here was me thinking that you was mister high and mighty. But I have to tell you, I'm sorry the way it's all turned out. I thought once that I'd like to hear that you had got your comeuppance, but I only feel sorry. You poor bugger, nobody deserves that."

"Can't you get a piece on the side?" Pete asked. "So you aren't so sexually frustrated?"

"Do you think I haven't tried?" Mac replied. "Tell me guys, am I so bad looking, or what? And be honest."

Mike made a big show of looking Mac over. "Well, all in all, I reckon that you'd pass for normal in the dark! The truth is Mac, you're quite a good-looking guy. So what's the problem?"

"The problem is that every woman I take to bed for sex never comes back for more."

Pete guffawed. "Perhaps you do it to them from the back

instead of the front. Most of them claim they don't like that." He laughed again. "That's why they don't come *back* for more. Get it? Back for more. *Backside*. Get it?"

"Yes, you puerile idiot," Mac said savagely. "I get it. Your sick and stupid humor is the same as when you were a bloody kid."

Looking around the restaurant, Mike tried to make sure that nobody could overhear their conversation. As his eyes swept the room, he once again made abrupt eye contact with the old man. Despite the distance and the tables between them, he had the clear and distinct feeling that the old man had heard every word that they had spoken, starting from the moment they had first sat at the table. Again, those eyes held his with so much intimacy and openness that he was suddenly and acutely embarrassed.

The old coot must be gay, he muttered to himself.

"Well now," said Gus, his eyes sweeping the table. "That leaves only one of us unaccounted for." His eyes settled on Mike. "You traveled a long way, Mike, so make it worthwhile."

Mike swallowed, thinking about the old man. What the hell! His secrets were nothing compared to Gus, or Mac, or poor Steve.

Taking a long swig from his Brown Bros. Chardonnay, he looked at the others pensively. "If you're waiting for me to come up with something worse than we've already heard, you're going to be disappointed. The simple fact is that I'm deliriously happy in my marriage to Tessa, and that after eighteen years, I'm the luckiest guy around so far as that is concerned. My two kids are great, and we have a good relationship between us. Good, but could be better. How to make that happen I've no idea. Dawn is fifteen now and into this new world of computers and electronic toys. I'm not even sure that we speak the same language. Billy is seventeen, and he's a good kid. Only trouble is we, too, seem to live in different worlds. But it's okay between us. Just, could be better."

"So, whose fault is that?" Pete asked.

"In all fairness, probably mine," Mike replied. "They think that Tessa and I are a bit odd, particularly me." He took a deep breath. "Ah well, in view of your honesty, I'll have to share something that I've hidden from you for a long time. You see, I'm totally committed to my spiritual path. I am on a journey into self. I want ... no, I *need* to know who I am. I have a longing to penetrate the mysteries of life; to know the meaning of life, to know the meaning of me." He looked mildly embarrassed.

"Tessa and I do a lot of meditation, and we go on spiritual retreats and to seminars. And, of course, we read a lot of that sort of books. Personally, I love visionary fiction." He felt the old enthusiasm surging through him. "Talk about vision, passion and action. It's great reading; you should try it."

The other four sat staring at Mike.

"Whatever are you prattling on about?" asked Pete.

"God! You're one of those new age cuckoos," said Gus.

"I don't think it's cuckoo," Steve said strongly. "It beats the shit out of my misery and just might provide an answer."

"I've read the same type of books," Mac said quietly, "and if there is anywhere that I can find any answers at all for my particular problems, I believe that's where I'll find them."

Mike looked both bemused and pleased. "Well, I am surprised. Two of you think I'm nuts, and that's okay, and two of you are open to a different way. Two out of four is far, far better than I expected."

"Sorry, Mike, but it's looney tunes so far as I'm concerned," Pete said. "You have my profound sympathy that you can be so bloody gullible. Hell, I have to arrest people like you for sit-down strikes and all that sort of bullshit."

Mike laughed. "Talk about lumping everything that doesn't fit the status quo into one barrel. Personally, I have never been involved in a sit-down strike to protest some controversial governmental or environmental issue or whatever; but Billy, who really shuns what Tess and I are into, has been involved in several. He even got arrested once, and I had to bail him out."

"I hope you really chewed him out," growled Pete.

"No, I didn't. Actually, I told him that I was really rather proud of him, that he had so much commitment to an issue. What that particular protest was about escapes my memory, but he did show a passion that I rather enjoyed. The odd thing is, he does not like the same passion in me."

"Perhaps he doesn't recognize where it comes from." Steve said sagely.

Mike looked at him in surprise, his eyebrows high. "Yes, I think you could be right. Given time, we could be on the same wavelength. Thanks for the insight, Steve."

Steve gave an embarrassed mumble. "Wish I could help myself as easily."

A new voice caught them all by surprise, and it was softly spoken, but it carried such an intensity they were left with the feeling that the words might well have come from within themselves. Each word penetrated their consciousness, cutting through their personal haze of thoughts with ease and formidable power.

"You could, Steve. So, indeed, could all of you. And, if you will permit me, I will teach you how."

Five pairs of startled eyes shot up, focusing on the elderly gentleman who stood regarding them from the end of the table.

Mike blinked in astonishment. Only seconds earlier he had been aware of the old guy sitting at his own table. Now he was here, with them. How did he manage that, unseen? What was going on?

CHAPTER THREE

MANY WAYS OF BEING

Gee!" Mike spluttered foolishly, and he put no thought into how his surprise would be received. "How in the name of all that's holy did you get from your table to here?"

"Who bloody cares," growled Pete. "Bloody cheek. Buzz off, old-timer, before I bloody arrest you."

The old man smiled at Pete, but his eyes were blue ice. "For what reason, my lugubrious friend? For offering timely assistance?"

"Don't push it, or I'll find a reason," Pete muttered.

"Do so, my friend, and your problem with promotion will be replaced with problems of demotion."

Rising to his feet, Pete towered over the elderly man. "Are you threatening me, old man?"

The elderly man sadly shook his head, his eyes sweeping and holding them all, one by one. "Allow me to introduce myself. My name is Deliverance, and that is what I offer you. However, say the word, and I will leave you now, never to return."

Pete grinned nastily. "Fine, the word is, piss off."

The old man gave a slight bow, turning on his heels, but in that moment Mike leapt to his feet and placed himself before the old man.

"Wait ... please. Pete doesn't speak for me." He looked anxiously at the others. "Or for all of us. Please stay ... I just feel it's important."

Indicating the single empty chair next to him, and not quite sure of why he was doing so, Mike continued to try and soothe

the situation. “I’m speaking from instinct only, and I’m uncertain of what I’m saying, but I do know that I want to hear you out. I’m intrigued.”

“Intuition, not instinct,” the old man said with a smile.

“Huh?” Mike looked puzzled. “I don’t get it.”

“I know. That’s why I have offered my services. But just for the record, humans are intuitive, animals are instinctive.”

“Oh.” Mike was floundering uncomfortably.

“Did you say that your name is Deliverance?” Steve asked, “or did I dream that.”

“You were awake for my name, yes. It’s the rest of your life that is a dream,” the old man replied.

“And what do you propose to deliver us from?” Gus asked.

“Your dreams, or should I say, living nightmares. Your helplessness, inadequacy, your frustrations. Your basic ignorance about life.”

“Hey, steady on with how you describe us,” Pete scowled.

“Your own word, for yourself, was inadequate,” the old man reminded him. ”However, I certainly have not come here to banter words with you. Do you want deliverance from the mess your lives have become, or would you rather they continue to follow the way that they currently are heading? I am going to leave you for ten minutes. Think about what I have said, and talk it over among yourselves.”

As the old man made to stand up, Mac reached out and grabbed the gentleman’s arm.

“Not so fast. I have a few questions to ask before I even know what to think about this deliverance business. I know this sounds stupid and even melodramatic, but I have to ask, are you in league with the devil? Are we expected to sell you our souls for your help? And if you really want to help us, what’s in it for you?”

The old man rose to his feet, Mac’s hand falling away as though suddenly burnt. He looked at Mac with a sad expression.

"I suppose such questions are inevitable, but I really thought better of you. I will be generous and assume it is the drink speaking. I am not in league with the devil. The very opposite would be more accurate. As for your souls! Tell me, what do you know of your souls? And what is in it for me? That I can easily tell you. Joy! Upliftment. And incredible fulfillment. These are what I experience when I teach people like you how to find and use their inner power."

His eyes locked with Mike, a smile on his face as he spoke quietly. "Never doubt that you have power."

For an endless moment, it seemed that Mike was staring into blue space. Somewhere in his thoughts he knew that these were just eyes ... until he noticed the stars. He saw an impossible distant figure walking toward him from across the gulf of starlight. As the figure came closer, he paused, throwing a ball of white light toward Mike. Spinning toward him, the ball unraveled itself into letters, in turn becoming a single word, a word formed from light, a word he could both see and, from within, hear — *Believe.*

He blinked in bewilderment. The old man was moving from the table and across the room as smoothly as if he was moving back into the light and space among the stars.

Mike sat shocked. Was that real? Did the others see it? He glanced at them, knowing instantly that it had been for his eyes only.

He looked at the others, dazed. "My God."

"Just your average fruit cake," Pete said wearily. "The world's full of them. And I should know, they occupy half my time. When he comes back, we simply tell him to get lost."

Mike shook his head. "That may be your reality, but it isn't mine. I think he really has something to offer us. There is something very different about him. Something mystical. I just ... somehow, er, saw him in space."

"Space!" Pete laughed derisively. "Man, is he getting to you, or what? Like I said, he's a fruit cake. And what's this about my reality and yours? Is this the new age language shit?"

Mike grinned, nodding his head.

"I guess it is. In my life, or my reality, it's possible to meet someone like Deliverance who is somehow way beyond the normal. Mind you, it is also extremely unlikely for this to happen, very rare, but not impossible. I guess that in your reality it's either impossible or unacceptable. Deliverance has already proved that he's not impossible, so for you he must be unacceptable. That's a real limitation."

"Anyway, how can anyone have a name like Deliverance?" Mac asked. "I mean, whoever heard of a name like that?"

"We did, just now," Steve said. "Personally, I'm all for hearing the guy out. Let's face it, what would happen if he had said his name was Jesus? Would we feel better, or reassured? Or would we call him a religious nut and be just as unbelieving?"

"I would've arrested him, that's what would have happened." Pete said mildly. "Can't have known criminals running around."

"You mean the Bible was wrong?" Mike mocked. "Jesus was a known criminal?"

Pete gave him a superior smirk. "Actually, according to the laws of that time, yes, he was a known criminal."

Mike nodded reluctantly. "Yeah, I set that one up and then walked straight into it. Gee, isn't it something when the law is more criminal than the crooks? However, suppose Jesus reappeared, now, as a guy named Deliverance?"

"Shit! Are you kidding me?" Pete looked incredulous.

Mike shrugged. "Well, let's vote on it. But let me be clear. If you guys don't want to talk with him any further, I do, and I shall tell him so. As far as I'm concerned, there is something magical about Deliverance, and I want more. So, is it us, or just me?"

"What makes you say magical? Odd maybe, even weird, but why magical?" Steve asked.

Mike felt embarrassed. "Well, I know you won't believe this, but just before he walked away, I looked into his eyes, and I saw space ... a space filled with stars."

"You mean like outer space?" Gus asked with a smirk.

Mike squirmed, but doggedly continued. "Yeah, I do. Anyway, I saw this figure, all illuminated walking toward me, then he threw me a ball of light. As it flew from his hand, it unraveled into a word." He paused, feeling vulnerable and stupid.

"So," Steve said. "What was the word?"

"Believe," Mike said in a small voice.

Pete roared with laughter. "In a rat's arse. I don't know who the biggest nut is, you or him. You can count me out of this fiasco."

"Mike, are you telling us the truth?" Steve asked.

Mike sighed. "You have my word that I'm telling you exactly what I experienced. It doesn't help to tell you that the figure in space was Deliverance, but I just know it was."

"Right, I want to hear what he has to say," Steve said firmly.

"I'm intrigued," Mac said. "Look me in the eyes, Mike, and tell me again that you are not kidding around."

"I'm telling you the truth. It's what I experienced. Honestly," Mike said, looking at Mac.

"Well, I may be a sucker, but you can count me in," Mac said. "It'll be entertaining, if nothing else."

Gus shrugged. "I have to admit, right or wrong, I believe Mike is sincere." He sighed. "*Believe* ... what an odd thing to say ... if it happened! If he was making it up, I would have expected Mike to say something more exotic. Okay, I'll believe you. Anyway, I've always liked the Twilight Hour on television. So, what's to lose? I'm in."

They all looked at Pete.

Pete shook his head angrily. "I can't believe that this is happening. If the lads at the station got to hear about this, I'd be the laughing stock. To hell with all of you, I'm off. And be very sure that this is the last of our reunions that I'll be at."

Getting to his feet, Pete glared at each of them. "Some friends you turned out to be."

That said, he walked out of the restaurant swiftly, the others sitting stunned by the speed of his reaction and withdrawal.

Mike shook his head vigourously. "Did we tell him to get lost, or did I miss it? My God, what a reaction."

"Seems like his life is dominated by what the lads might think," Steve said. "Gee, and I thought I had problems."

"I am sorry if I have caused a split among you."

The voice, though soft, again cut through everything with powerful insistence, engaging their attention. Unnoticed, the elderly man had returned.

Steve recovered first. "It's not your fault, old ... er ... um, Deliverance. Too many years have passed for us to remain as close as we were. We've all grown apart, and being in the police force, Pete has developed certain restrictions."

"To be fair, I think they are his, rather than inherited from the police," Deliverance said.

"Even as a kid he needed to be needed," Mike added. "I remember when he was banished from the gang. It was a dreadful punishment for him. Of course, we took him back again. But it's a pity now, he's a good guy under it all."

"I don't want to be out of order," Mac said determinedly, "but did Mike really see what he told us he saw? About stars and space," he finished lamely.

Deliverance smiled at him. "Believe," he said.

Shocked, Mac and Gus stared at each other.

"Right, I'm convinced," Mac said, challenging the others.

"Yeah, that is one hell of a clincher," Gus added.

Steve nodded. "We're with you, but I still want to know how someone gets a name like Deliverance. Did you inherit it, adopt it, or was it actually a birth name? Like John Deliverance."

The old man sat at the table and glanced around. "It seems likely that we will be here for some time yet. You will notice that most of the other patrons have gone, but do not worry. I own this restaurant. It serves a very useful purpose. Strange as it may seem, in this vicinity when people like yourselves want, or should I say, need me in their lives, they often come along here for a meal." He laughed softly. "And sometimes what they get is hard for them to digest."

"As in Pete," Mike said.

"Yes, as in Pete. But each person must be free to choose his way, and your friend has chosen. For your sake, Mac, I will explain how I have my name, so listen carefully."

Making himself comfortable, Deliverance gazed at each one of them as though gauging their various levels of involvement and comprehension.

"In the stream of human consciousness, there are many basic principles. I call them the Principles of Truth. Honor is one, trust another, integrity, respect and acceptance are others. There are more, but if you are expressing true honor in your daily living, you will find that most other principles are satellites zipping around it," he continued.

"We each come into life with a certain unrecognized mission. It is simple enough to do, but we make it complicated, as with everything else we do. That mission is first and foremost to make ourselves more of what we are and less of what we are not. Unfortunately, most people manage to make a complete mess of this, with the reverse happening as their result."

Steve held up his hands. "Whoa, whoa, slow down. You've lost me. Did I hear you right? We should make ourselves more of what we are and less of what we are not?"

Deliverance nodded. "That is correct."

"But what does it mean, for Chrissake?" Mac asked.

"To make yourself more of what you are means that you should live in a way that focuses on, and develops, the inherent magnificence, wisdom and joy that we all are, that we all contain. A focus on these in your daily life, and they develop and express. To reverse this process, you focus instead on the mundane, the negatives and the problems of life. This, people do easily. Nobody needs teaching."

Steve shook his head. "I'm not sure that I get it."

"Do you criticize yourself or other people?"

Steve's expression went wry. "Sure. Who doesn't?"

"I do not." Deliverance said. "And if I did, I would have nothing to offer you. Every criticism is a focus away from magnificent toward the mundane. To criticise, you are required to look at what isn't as you think it should be. I am suggesting that you replace it with a real appreciation for what is as you think it should be.

"However, we are getting sidetracked here. It is imperative that the principles I mentioned are anchored and expressed in the human consciousness. For this reason, there are those of us who, having reached a specific level of attainment, have chosen to express and embody one, or even a number, of these principles. Not surprisingly, I embody and express deliverance. In other words, when the pupil is ready ... I deliver." He smiled. "I also encourage."

"I have never heard of anything like that." Mac said, frowning.

"I believe you," Deliverance replied. "It is obvious, but do not worry about it. You have a lot of company."

"Yeah, like me," Steve said with a grin.

"And me, almost," Mike intoned. "What I mean is, I've heard and read of such things, but I've never encountered the reality. Until now. So where do we go from here?"

"Well, for a start, I can only deliver where there is a true willingness to receive. So, how is it with you boys?"

"I'm in." Mike said firmly. "I only wish Tessa was here. Personally, I reckon that this is the opportunity of a lifetime. I have to pinch myself to be sure that it's real."

"Count me in," said Steve. "When you've been up shit-house creek as long as I have, you don't turn anything down. Besides, crazy as it seems, I believe in you."

"I'm open to what you have to say," Mac said. "Or at least, I hope I am! It all makes a strange kind of sense so far."

Mike looked at Gus. "You've been quiet for a long time, Gus. What are your feelings? Are you open to Deliverance becoming a sort of teacher for us?"

Gus took a deep breath, letting it out slowly and noisily.

"I've been listening, believe me, and I'm in somewhat of a dilemma. Personally, I want to believe in what seems to be happening, but my whole background, my beliefs, even the fading echoes of my religion, are all against it. I'm not even sure I can oppose all that, even if I want to."

Deliverance smiled into his eyes. "I'm sorry, Gus, truly sorry, but you do have to choose. It is crucial to the process. Just going along with it is not good enough."

Gus nodded, sighing. "Yeah. I can appreciate that. It's stupid, isn't it? Look at me. Did you ever see anyone more in need of help? Do you think that I don't know I'm a heart attack waiting to happen? To be honest, I don't ... didn't ... care. I figured that there would be less pain dead than alive." He looked Deliverance in the eyes. "Are you saying that there is really and truly a chance for me? Could I really turn this ... this total failure of a life into something grand, magnificent?"

Deliverance nodded. "Yes, you can if you choose that you can. And if you live that choice."

Gus coughed on his cigar smoke. "I suppose that means no more cigars?"

"Do they honor your lungs, your body? Do they honor the magnificent you?"

"I get your point," Gus replied, "but they are really good at deadening the pain."

"Even better at deadening your body," Deliverance said.

"What I need is something miraculous," Gus said wistfully.

"It just so happens that I can offer you something miraculous," Deliverance replied. I can give you a magic formula, but first you have to put some of the basics in place. Then, a daily dose of the magic formula, and your life can be happy and fulfilled."

"Truly?" Gus asked. "Or are you having me on?"

"Truly," Deliverance said smiling. "It's my speciality. I have devised a fail-safe formula that works like magic. But, and there is always a but, you have to use it, and apply it, daily."

"That's all?" said Gus, his face lighting up. "In that case, I'm in with the other guys. If you think that I'm not a lost cause, that's good enough for me."

"Gus," Deliverance said, "hear me. If *you* think that you are a lost cause, then you are right, you are. If *you* think that you are not a lost cause, that you are truly worthwhile, then that is true also. It is not what I think that matters in your life or what anyone else thinks about you. Your life is made up of what you think and believe about yourself. Make your decision. Are you a lost cause, or are you worthwhile?"

"I'm bloody worthwhile," Gus said smiling, as though he had just been released from hell. "Bloodied and battered, but definitely worthwhile." He beamed at the others.

"Wow! If this don't beat all," Steve whooped.

"Er, I get the somewhat belated feeling that we should introduce ourselves to you. Not as a formality, but just so you know a bit more about us," Mike suggested.

"I appreciate the offer, but I already know the details," Deliverance said. "Allow me, Michael Edward Ward, forty-nine years into this life, working in sustainable ecosystems for your local council. Married to Tessa, a supermarket manager. You have two children. Need I continue?" Deliverance asked.

"Then we have Murray Macray, better known as Mac, forty-eight years, married to Betty, a childhood sweetheart, and currently separated, with one boy of eighteen still at school. You are a professor of English literature.

"Steven David Alec Wright, forty-six years, and unmarried. You were in the merchant marines for twenty years, quit, and have been without a steady job for six years. Finally, there is Anthony James Edwards, forty-nine years, mostly known as Gus. A draughtsman, married to Harriet, with two daughters, Jennifer and Amanda, fourteen and fifteen years respectively. There is more, of course, for all of you, but I think this is sufficient to indicate that I know your history."

"How the hell do you know all this?" Steve scowled.

"Oh, I know more. Those are just the normal statistics. I also know some of what goes on in your heads."

Steve pulled his shoulders back, sitting up straighter.

"That's okay by me. If you know how I got up shit-house creek, you should be able to teach me how to paddle out of it. That, I can handle, but how the hell do you know all those things about us? It ain't natural."

Gus, Mike and Mac nodded their agreement.

Deliverance sighed. "It's easy enough, boys. Let's take a simple Truth and look at it. Consciousness draws to Self form — that is, a physical body — through which to express. And the expression is consciousness. This means that your body, your soul — *you* — are an expression of consciousness. Are you with me?"

Gus shook his head and blinked. "Give me a moment to think about it. The booze doesn't help."

"That's for sure," Deliverance replied. "How about the rest of you? Is it clear?"

"You know it isn't, don't you?" Mike said shrewdly. "You know in the same way as you know all about us."

Deliverance nodded approvingly. "Very good. Look at it this way. We are each a conscious Being. That consciousness, which is who you are, is a frequency. And within that frequency is a record of our whole life in every finest detail. For a person who is highly attuned to such vibrations, it is not difficult to read. It is rather in the manner of listening to an inner voice."

"That's just a little bit like saying that we are each a CD and that the CD is a frequency of consciousness. When you play it and listen to that frequency, you know what is on the CD," Mike suggested.

Deliverance clapped his hands and laughed. "Excellent. You have stated it perfectly."

Steve, Mac and Gus looked at Mike in astonishment.

"Say, that's good, Mike. Now, I get it." Steve turned toward Deliverance. "You can tune into people in the way I listen to a CD or radio station, so of course you know our loony tunes." He looked at Gus and Mac. "You guys both get it, huh?"

Gus nodded. "Put like that, of course."

Mac looked thoughtful. "That would be a formidable skill for a politician to have. Just imagine what he could do."

"You need never worry about that happening," Deliverance laughed. "It does not go with the political territory. The person who learns such skills can only employ them in a way that benefits the whole, not the few."

Gus shook his head. "You just lost me again."

"At this point, you need not be concerned," Deliverance stated. "But just for the record, politics deals with life on the mundane level, believing that all things are separate. They inadvertently focus on creating problems, then they attempt to solve them. This is considered normal. I focus on Truth, and by revealing it in a person's life, allow him to resolve the illusions of separation."

"I feel like a bloody idiot," Mac sighed, "but I just got lost again. I get the bit about the politicians. That's clear, because we all do the same things in our daily lives. It's the bit about separation and wholeness and illusions that loses me."

Nodding patiently, Deliverance settled back. "Okay, just listen from the heart. This may take a while, so do not struggle to understand. Just listen, and let us see what happens."

CHAPTER FOUR

A MEETING WITH TRUTH

"What you focus on in your daily life is what you get," Deliverance explained. "Most people seem to think that they understand this, but few really do. For example, if you have a problem and focus on solving that problem, come up with the solution and then apply it, most people would then expect that the problem is finished with."

"But, of course," Mac said, "that's common sense."

Deliverance shook his head. "You see? Mac thinks that he understands. He calls that common sense while, in the way of Truth, I call it nonsense. The way that Mac sees it is the way that it appears to be. But, boys, I am here to tell you that people's lives generally are in a mess because truly nothing really is as it appears to be. Let me take the problem-solving as a classic example. If you focus on your problem, looking for resolution, your focus is the problem. So, you solve the problem, but the focus remains, and the focus is *problem*. Not *a* problem, or *the* problem, but simply problem. Does it not seem obvious by now that if problem is the focus, then problem remains, and the whole problem cycle will begin, or rerun, all over again?

"Now, let us put this into a governmental situation. What is the overall, primary focus of any government anywhere in the world?"

After a few moments of silence, Gus said, "Problems."

"Exactly. And no governing body will ever solve them, because inadvertently their focus continually is based in the manifestation of problems. This, of course, is not their exclusive domain. It is happening in almost every family on a global scale." He sighed.

"And very few of them would even take the time to investigate what I have just told you. It would be rejected outright. As indeed, you may so do, yourselves."

"Not me," Mike said. "I'm vaguely familiar with what you have said, and I do see the problem."

Gus gave a great yell, "Idiot! Did you hear yourself?"

Mike looked sheepish. "Yeah, I did. And that wasn't deliberate. My God! It's so deeply ingrained."

Mac chuckled. "No problem here."

"To state I do not have a problem is no different from the statement of having a problem," Deliverance said quietly. "The focus is still problem. Forget the governmental situations, what is it that you — personally — most focus on in your life? This means, in effect, what is it that you most think about and talk about?"

As Deliverance sat back reflectively, Mike studied him. He was of medium height, slim, with quite unremarkable features. His fair hair was very short, thinning, his face strong and calm. His blue eyes that were very direct held your attention, while the thrust of his jaw declared that this was a man with a strong sense of purpose. Overall, he gave the impression he was at peace with himself and the world.

"That's easy. I think more about my problems than anything, but I also think about their resolution," Steve said.

"And what is your emotional state as you think about your problems?" Deliverance asked.

"Anxiety. Hopelessness. Despair," Steve replied.

"And the rest of you?" Deliverance asked.

"Me too," said Gus.

"And me," said Mac, with a glum face.

"No," said Mike, "that's not me. I don't consider that I have any real problems. I focus mostly on my journey into life, and on Tessa and the kids. My work also gets a fair bit of attention, depending on how interesting the current project is."

Deliverance smiled at him. "That's good to hear." He looked at the other three. "Okay guys, let us look at what Steve has said. First, he called them *my problems*. This means that he identifies himself with his problems, claiming ownership of them. This is all done in a state of anxiety, hopelessness and despair. Is that a fair summary?"

The others nodded reluctantly. "Put like that, I can see that it's a nasty picture," Steve mumbled.

Mac and Gus nodded soberly.

"Unfortunately, it does create rather a nasty reality," Deliverance said, nodding.

He sat staring at them for a few moments, as though looking into their very souls.

"Er ... can I buy you a drink ... or anything?" Mike asked.

Deliverance chuckled. "I sell it, son. I do not drink it. But thank you for the offer. How about you boys? I think that some strong coffee would be appropriate about now."

They all nodded vigourously, murmuring appreciation.

Turning away from them, Deliverance gestured, and a blonde woman they had not seen before waved back from the far end of the room. Holding up four fingers, Deliverance lifted his hand high.

Turning toward them again, he shook his head, a small, mischievous smile playing around his lips. "If you boys get into this seriously, I will take it a bit deeper. But, for now, just pay attention to what might be a whole new line of thought and speculation for you. To any thinking person, it must be obvious that there is a purpose in life for humanity. We are reasoning, creative Beings.

What is not quite so obvious is that there are universal laws governing this creativity.

"The first and foremost of these is so simple, but devastating in its impact. We are required to live and experience what we create." He shook his head. "No way round it, no way out, but so few people realize it. Another of these laws that is also completely overlooked, unrealized, is equally simple: there is no time off from creativity.

"Think about what I have said for a moment. We must live and experience the very substance of what we create, and there is no time off from creating."

Deliverance stopped speaking for several minutes while the impact of his words sank in.

"Another law of creation to ponder: our thoughts and words are the focus for our creation. In other words, what we most think about is what we create. Can you easily see the foundation of human suffering in all this? The vast majority of people think and talk about the things that they least want in their lives. People think more about what they do *not* want in their lives than what they *do* want." He shook his head sadly. "They call that human nature, but it is not. It is the habit of hopelessness."

Deliverance sat back and smiled at the blonde woman who had just approached the table, a large tray in her hands.

"Thank you, Elsie. Much appreciated." He smiled at her fondly as she quietly withdrew.

"Okay, boys. There is strong, black coffee in the dark jug, creamy milk in the white one, and hot water in the glass jug. Pour it how you like it. And there is sugar or honey if you like it sweet."

Mike took his black, but watered down and unsweetened, while Mac and Gus opted for strong and creamy, with lashings of brown sugar.

Deliverance waited until they were all sipping contentedly.

"Any comments? Any questions?"

"You spell it out pretty clearly," Gus commented, "but I would like some explanation on what you mean when you say that there is no time off from creating."

"What it means, boys, is that every thought you have is creative. And creative thought eventually manifests into a physical expression. That physical expression happens to be our life. In other words, we each create our own reality, and hardly anyone is aware of doing so. In fact, many people would mock the very idea of what I am talking about."

He paused for a moment, looking keenly at the others.

"And yet, it continues. Mocked or accepted, it continues."

"So, are you saying that while I think about and talk about my life as being a complete shit-house, then I am continually creating that reality? The fact that I don't want it means nothing. I'm creating a reality that I don't want," said Steve.

Deliverance nodded. "You got it. Your thoughts and words continually reinforce and maintain the reality that you created, continue to create, but do not want."

Steve shook his head in amazement. "Gee! If that don't beat all. But how come people don't know about this?"

"Because people ignore Truth."

"You talk a lot about Truth," Mac said, "but what is it? I mean, is there a single liberating Truth or is it an amalgam of many small Truths? How do you define it?"

Deliverance stared at Mac thoughtfully for several minutes. Finally, he nodded.

"That is a good question. I only wish the answer would be as simple to understand as it is to say. First of all, there is a timing to Truth. You may see it differently, but it was you boys who brought this meeting into your lives. I did not come to your table uninvited, as an intruder. I came at your invitation to deliver change into your lives. One of you was so out of touch with his inner cry for help that he walked away, while the rest of you who remained touched into some deep awareness of the need for change. Despite not being aware of it, you boys responded to the timing of your unrealized cries for help. For Pete, the timing was not that precise. Do you understand what I am saying?"

Mike nodded. "Yeah. I was connecting with you long before you came to our table. Your eyes, your whole energy, seemed to draw me like a magnet. I guess that I was feeling the timing on deeper levels, yet I had no intellectual awareness of this." He laughed. "To be honest, I was rather threatened by the connection between us. Not frightened, but threatened."

"I was aware of this," Deliverance said, nodding.

"I think I see what you mean about timing," Mac said, "but I'm still in the dark about Truth."

"That sums it up for me, too," Gus agreed.

"Okay, listen. If Truth reveals itself in the framework of timing, then it will be recognized and invariably acted upon. If it is not the timing for Truth, then it either passes by, unnoticed, or it is disregarded, dismissed as nonsense."

"But what is Truth?" Mac asked insistently.

"Truth is life meeting you in the moment, revealing itself. That is Truth."

"But ... but ... I thought that Truth would be some profound and revealing statement that could change lives," Gus said, a look of disappointment on his face.

Mike laughed. "Are you kidding? Are you dumb, or what? How much more profound can it get? Did you hear what he said? Truth is life ... meeting you in the moment ... and revealing itself. Man! That is deep. I need time for that to sink in and percolate through my heart."

"Bravo," Deliverance applauded. "Percolate through the heart it is, not through the brain. The heart knows Truth, but to the brain it is a stranger. Truth always reveals its presence through the heart, the seat of the soul."

"I have to confess, I do feel for what you are saying," Mac said, nodding. "If I think about your statement on Truth, I get lost. It's as though my brain doesn't know what to do with it or where to go, but my heart does. In my heart I can feel that statement singing. It feels like an unfamiliar but very welcomed light. I like the feeling."

"To be honest, I'm still back there struggling with the concept that I'm the one creating the mess in my life," Steve declared. "I mean, I knew that I was doing it wrong and that it was my fault, but I also felt that life was a bummer and out to get me. Every day was another battle to survive. That was my life. It knocks the shit outta me to even approach the idea that I did all this to myself." He glanced sideways at Deliverance, uncertainly. "You are sure about all this, aren't you? I mean, could you be wrong?"

Deliverance smiled wryly. "It is Truth. But, is it your timing to be able to accept it and then act upon it?"

Steve nodded slowly, frowning. He sighed. "Yeah. It's my time. I hear you and, deep down, I get it. I'm just shocked that I created the total stuff-up of my life."

"The reality is, your life is not a stuff-up," Deliverance said. "You have simply brought yourself into a very creative place and time in your life. You can, if you now choose, bring Truth into your life. The fact that you have lived with such a poor self-image, creating stress, anxiety, all the emotional suffering, humiliation, etcetera, means that you will now pay deep and respectful attention to this present opportunity. Had I responded to your inner call while you were riding on a crest of success, do you think that you would have heeded me?"

"Hell, I'm not even sure that I would have needed you."

Deliverance laughed. "Oh, you would have needed me, right enough, but you certainly would not have known that. And had I come in answer to your unrealized call, what would you have done?"

"Dismissed you as a nutter, a crank."

"Exactly. So, do you see that you are, in fact, better off in your present situation, as you begin a new journey, than you would have been, lost in the hypothetical one? Desperation opens doorways, complacency closes them. And, let me add, that the latter situation is not a hypothetical one for a great number of so-called successful people. They pay a far higher price than is ever realized. They seldom discover that the costly prestige and comfort they crave is paid for by much more than money. Comfort attracts complacency, and from that potent but negative relationship, stagnation is given birth. It almost invariably takes something dramatic to break a person's attachment to their comfort."

He looked at Steve musingly. "If I told you that your past several lives involved great wealth, and that in this lifetime you have been creating exactly the drama needed to break out of the stagnation that those lives created, would you still feel such a total failure?"

Steve looked utterly astonished. "Past lives! I've heard of the concept, but I've never given it any credibility. Do you mean to tell me that we do live a number of lives, that we come back, over and over, like in some of the movies I've seen?"

Deliverance sighed quietly. "If you were to accept the reality of past lives, then consider my question. Would you feel better about yourself knowing that you were breaking away from the stagnation of your past?"

"To be honest, of course I would. Who wouldn't?"

"Who, indeed," Deliverance said patiently. "Then accept a small gift from me, for that is your reality."

Steve's jaw hung open. "You *are* serious?"

"Very."

Grinning, Steve said, "I accept. Wow!" He punched the air. "Yeah!"

"Could you convince me about all this past lives stuff?" Gus asked. "Because I'm seriously sceptical about it."

Deliverance glanced at his wristwatch. "No more tonight, boys. It's now two-fifteen in the morning. I suggest that we meet here tomorrow night at eight o'clock. Be my guests for dinner."

He grinned at Gus. "I have no interest in convincing you of anything, my friend, but I will explain *one life* to you and what that really means. What you accept, believe, and do with it is entirely up to you."

CHAPTER FIVE

AND SO IT BEGINS

Mike had been on the phone talking to Tessa for quite a while, telling her about the unexpected death of Lenny, and Pete's abrupt departure. Now he was pleading his case for extra time. It had been agreed between them that he would be traveling home one full day after the gang of six had met. From experience, he knew that he would need a day to recover from his usual hangover headache. He always intended to drink moderately, but when he was with the others, he invariably consumed more wine than he could handle. Now, everything was suddenly changed. He was hoping that Deliverance would meet with them each evening for at least another week.

"You are sure that you are not having me on, with this Deliverance character?" Tessa insisted. "He sounds very unlikely."

"Darling, he's real, I assure you. Have I ever made up a story like this before? And to what purpose? I love you and I can't wait to get home to be with you. But how can I pass an opportunity like this? The man is ... I don't know how to describe him. He's like a modern sage. Yeah! That says it well. It's like he walked out of nowhere, just for us."

"But you said that he owns the restaurant."

"Yes, he does. But he, the man, is shrouded in mystery. He looks about sixty something, yet he calls us boys, as though he is vastly older. I'm going to ask him about that."

"Well, all right my love," Tessa agreed, "but you will have to teach me all that you have learned when you get home. Give me a phone call every morning so I can have a summary while it's still fresh in your memory. And give Deliverance — that really is an odd name — many thanks from me. It's nice of him to care."

"You know, you're right, he really does care. It comes across, even though he seems a bit strict."

"He would need to be strict with a bunch of blokes like you," Tessa said with a laugh. "Strict and patient! Oh, by the way, what about your work situation?"

"I've already phoned Bert and told him that I'm going to be delayed for a week or so. He said not to worry. They are not overly busy right now, so it's not a problem."

"You make sure you phone me daily," Tessa said with mock severity. "This *or so* tacked on after a week away isn't going to get a good reception."

Mike chuckled. "You just keep that supermarket running, and the time will be gone before you know it."

"Hmmm, we'll see. Anyway, I've got to go. Take care, my darling, I love you. And be a good boy! Bye."

Mike found that the day dragged as he impatiently waited for the evening to arrive. The others were at work, and he wondered what he could do to occupy himself. One day in the city had been all he wanted of that, and apart from another day in the museums or an occasional movie, he would have to find something to do.

He arrived at The Offbeat Eatery at around a quarter past seven that evening, deciding to have a drink while he waited. Walking over to the small bar, he realized for the first time that liquor was understated in this restaurant rather than promoted.

The bar was tasteful and quiet, with not a bottle to be seen. The bamboo effect created the feeling of a small summer house, and as he sat down in one of the comfortable chairs, he had the momentary impression that he was facing an open window with woodland views. A large, window-sized part of the wall had been cleverly recessed, and within that framework, the window and view had been artistically created by a vibrant mural. The overall result was both enchanting and very realistic.

Mike ordered himself a grapefruit juice, having no wish to follow the previous night's excess. As he sucked on the black straw, his eyes swept the restaurant, finally realizing and appreciating that its whole decor was deliberately understated.

"Good evening, Mike. I am happy to see you again."

It was odd, Mike thought, but Deliverance looked happy to see him. He could *feel* it.

"It's great to be here. I'm looking forward to learning as much from you as I can." A sudden, preposterous thought bubbled to the surface of his mind. "Er, is it possible that I could work here with you, er ... for you, for a week, or so? Or, er ... for as long as you are teaching us?"

Deliverance beamed at him, nodding. "Of course. As a matter of fact, I was going to suggest it. A week or so, at the most. We must not upset Tessa. I suggest that you move in here to sleep in one of my spare rooms and that you do a little work for your food and board. How does that sound?"

Mike was delighted. "That's great. Wonderful. Thank you."

Deliverance smiled. "Your room is ready. If you go quickly now, you can take my car to your hotel, settle up, collect your things and be back here by the time the others arrive. You have my assurance they will all be late."

Mike stared at him, bewildered. "How can you know all this? You knew already. And them being late, how do ... ?"

Deliverance cut him off, holding out the keys. "Go."

Sure enough, when Mike breathlessly arrived back at twenty-five past eight, the others had only recently taken their seats around the table that had been reserved for them and made their choices for their evening meal. The waiters were busy at other tables, and

Deliverance asked him for his choice from the extensive menu. A quick glance was enough. "A seafood salad for me," Mike said decisively. Looking at the others, he smiled his greetings. "What have you guys chosen?" he asked.

"We are all having a rare pepper steak, along with baked spuds and sour cream, and broccoli cheese," Mac said. "Can't beat a good steak. Beats all your prissy seafood."

"That's a matter of opinion," Mike said, grinning.

Coming back to them, Deliverance sat at the end of the table, and in turn, looked each one in their eyes. "So, you all came back. You are all ready to move along the path of self-discovery, preparing the foundation for the magic formula." He nodded. "It's good. But I have a question for you. I know why Mike appeared to be late. But, you three, why were you late? I said be here at eight o'clock, not eighteen minutes past eight. Do you have good reasons for being late?"

Gus straightened up immediately, his anger flaring. "Just hang on a minute. Who the hell are you to demand an explanation? Or to demand anything, come to that. We're all adults here, and I expect to be treated like one. Not like some tardy little kid, by a teacher."

Deliverance looked at the others mildly. "Is that how you both feel?"

Steve shook his head. "No. I apologize. I was delayed in getting away." He shook his head. "Ah hell, I delayed myself. I'm always bloody late. No excuses." He looked directly at Deliverance. "But I would like to add that I meant no disrespect to you."

Deliverance's eyes twinkled as he looked at Mac.

Mac shrugged. "If you're going to make an issue of it, I'm always late, too. Doesn't matter how much I hurry, I'm always late. Sorry about that."

Looking at them steadily, Deliverance spoke in a soft voice that would not carry beyond their fairly secluded table. But he spoke with force and authority. "I am not interested in either apologies or excuses. Either you are here by eight o'clock tomorrow evening or do not even bother to walk in through that door. Do I make myself clear?"

His anger evaporated, Gus asked the question that really bugged him. "Why? I mean, why so exact on time? What difference does it make? Suppose I was a minute late, does that still apply?"

"It applies if you are one second late," Deliverance said. "Right now, I am considering whether to let the three of you just eat your meal, then go, or if to persist with you."

"I'd be grateful if you would persist," Steve said humbly.

Deliverance looked at him, the twinkle back in his eyes. "Having been asked with such a rare humility, I will. I will even tell you why I have made such an issue of this rather than just leave you to figure it out. Listen carefully, so we have no misunderstanding. Your lives — as you know and experience them — are made out of time: second by second, minute by minute, hour by hour, day by day, week by week, and so on. This is the substance of your life. Everything that you perceive yourself to be is formulated and made from the habits and conditioning of time. Are you with me?"

Everyone nodded vigourously.

"If, in the formation of your character you are always late for appointments, for meetings with people you care about and respect, for meetings with people whom you love, for special events in your life, you sow into your life the seed idea that you are not worthy of either their respect or of any respect for yourself. And as you continue to regularly be late — because it does not matter — so that *weed* seed germinates and grows, flourishing in the decay of your vanishing self-respect. As you lose your self-respect, so you gradually lose the threads of your life, and your life seems to become more random, more bad luck entering into it, and the path is downhill all the way. A pattern is established; a habit that, from such unrecognized beginnings, can be so very destructive in your life.

"You show me the person with truly good self-esteem and self-respect who has a downhill life and is always late for appointments and meetings with other people. Can you think of one such person in your life or an acquaintance?"

Gus and Mac tried hard to think of somebody, anybody, who fitted that description, finally giving up. Mike and Steve did not even bother. It all made too much sense.

"If you do not respect yourself, how can you respect other people? Being late is a subconscious, rather than a deliberately conscious way of letting other people know just where your life is at." Deliverance chuckled. "Dogs do their communicating about self-esteem by sniffing each others' anus. One sniff and they know the status, power and determination of that other dog. They know who is top dog — which they may challenge — and they know their standing in either a one-on-one or group relationship." He laughed. "We do it in a more subconscious way and on such a deep level that we ourselves are no longer aware of the messages that we are continually delivering, and receiving, from ourselves. But it happens, nevertheless.

"Mike arrived here early tonight. Nothing could have made him late, short of a so-called accident. I then sent him to get his things from the hotel he was staying in so that he can stay here for a week or so. I told him that you boys would all be late. And you were. Being late is part of the reality you have created in your lives." He shook his head slowly. "None of this makes you good or bad, right or wrong. It is simply the way that you have created and lived your lives. If you want this to change, it begins here. If you are late for our eight o'clock meetings, then you are not yet ready to take control of your lives." He looked at them all keenly, his face stern. "Are we all clear about this?"

They all nodded.

"I have a question," Mike began tentatively, "about age. You call us boys, and that feels okay, but you don't appear as more than, perhaps, twenty years older than us. That's the visual impression. But the *feeling* impression is one of much greater age. When we first met, we all thought of you as an old man, but that is not the visual impression. I'm not asking how old you are. I'm asking if my inner feeling is correct. That things are not quite as they seem."

Deliverance threw his head back, laughing heartily. "Oh Mike, if only you knew. One day, perhaps. Let me simply say that your inner feelings are correct and that you should always trust them. If those feelings ever let you down, you will usually find that it was your interpretation that was in error, not the basic feeling. Okay, boys, your meal will be here shortly, so I am going to begin with the issue we left last night: One life."

"But I thought that you said, or implied, that we have many lives," Gus interjected.

"Yes, we do," Deliverance said with a smile, "but each life is the continuity of One life. If you believe in a single life only, then your whole life will be based on a falsity. It is equally misguided and false if you base your belief in many lives, each one beginning and ending. I do not want to go in too deeply with this. For the changes that I want to promote in your lives right now, we need to keep to the basics. Who you are, let us say your soul self, is never born and never dies. On that soul level you are undying continuity. That soul expresses self through many bodies, each experiencing its own lifetime."

Seeing the somewhat blank faces on Steve, Mac and Gus, he laughed lightly. "The reality is not at all complicated. Okay, let us say that you have a movie on a video. The movie is made up of many thousands of frames, all joined in a sequence which makes visual sense. So, consider that the whole video is your soul life, while each frame of the movie is a physical body and identity lifetime. Does that make it easier?"

Gus and Mac nodded. "Yeah, I get it," Gus said, "but if it's true, how come this isn't common knowledge?"

"In many religions and philosophies it is common knowledge," Mike said.

Steve was looking thoughtful. "If this is the way of things," he said musingly, "then that means habits can easily migrate from one frame of the movie to the next. If I'm a loser in this life, this frame of the movie, then the chances are that it will continue. Right?"

Deliverance nodded. "Right."

"Christ!" said Mac feelingly. "How the hell do you get out of a habit that you don't know you have? I mean, how the hell can you stop something following you, when you don't know that you're being followed?"

"Truth knows, always. You just need to pay attention."

"What did you say Truth was?" Steve asked.

"May I?" Mike asked, looking at Deliverance.

"Sure, be my guest, son," Deliverance replied.

"I'm not trying to be smart," Mike said to the others, "but these words had such an impact on me I've been thinking about them most of the day. He said, Truth is life meeting you in the moment, revealing itself. What hit me so hard is that I'm seldom aware of the moment. My head is full of the future or the past, while the moment slips away unrealized."

Deliverance nodded. "You said it well, Mike. People think at the rate of several hundred words a minute. Unfortunately, most of that ... oh, look boys. Here comes your food."

The waiter arrived with their loaded plates balanced on a very large tray. He smiled respectfully at Deliverance. "Good evening, sir."

"It is indeed, George. It is indeed. And how is your wife?"

"Recovered, sir. And doing very well. She asked if she may speak with you soon."

"Of course she can, George. I will arrange it with her."

George nodded happily. "Thank you, sir."

While he was talking, George put a large and fully loaded plate before Gus, Mac and Steve, and a huge bowl of seafood salad before Mike. Although unordered, he placed a tall glass of grapefruit juice before each of them.

"*Bon appetit*," he murmured as he left.

Mike glanced at the empty place before Deliverance. "Er, aren't you eating with us?"

Deliverance smiled. "Today is not one of the days I eat. I do confess, however, that I have a great appreciation for fresh grapefruit juice."

Steve was already eating and smacked his lips with exaggerated gusto. "Man! This steak is good."

"Do you think you boys can eat and listen," Deliverance asked, "so we don't make it too late a night?"

He smiled as four heads nodded vigourously.

"Right, so let us begin with thinking, because it is something that people do, nonstop, all day. Your thinking creates your life. Hear me well, boys. Choose carefully what you think, because you will live what you choose."

Steve pulled a face. "Gee! My thoughts are trash."

"And what is your life?" Deliverance asked.

"Yeah. Trash!" Steve looked sad.

"There are many different problems in people's lives," Deliverance began, "but they do not all require different solutions. You boys, for example, have different problems, but to bring happiness and fulfillment into your lives requires each of you to respond to life in the same way. Many people believe that if you have wealth in your life you are successful. But I know a lot of very wealthy people, and the only problem that they do not have is money. They have a variety of relationship problems, self-esteem problems, emotional problems, sexual problems and health problems." He laughed. "And yet, just because they have money they are considered successful. Nothing could be further from the truth."

"So what would you call success?" Gus asked.

"To fully live your potential," Deliverance said slowly, looking at them each, in turn. "That is all it takes. It matters nothing what position you hold in life or who you are. All that is required from the soul Being you are is that you live your full potential. And although we all have different potential as physical Beings, we each have similar, unlimited potential as spiritual Beings."

For a while there was thoughtful silence.

CHAPTER SIX

FOOD FOR THOUGHT

Mac slowly chewed on his steak, his eyes seeing nothing as he savoured a moment of insight. "You're right," he said. "It makes sense. I've bought and read several books on wealth and success, and they were good books, but they only took it as far as ... as ... "

"Consensus reality can take it," Mike finished.

Mac gave him a puzzled look. "I was going to say as far as money can fix it, if that makes sense. I suppose consensus reality is part of your new age jargon."

"Not really. Consensus reality means that the vast majority of people see life in a way that is generally agreed as being the way it is. So consensus reality equates wealth with success, no matter that the person's private life may be a complete stuff-up," Mike explained.

"And I suppose if they suddenly lose that wealth, then they become an overnight failure," Gus added.

Mike nodded. "Yeah. That's how consensus reality would see it. Success is good, failure is bad — that's consensus reality. Everything is set out in rather concrete terms."

"So where do we go from here?" Steve asked.

They all looked at Deliverance.

Deliverance looked at them thoughtfully. "Well boys, as I said, what you think creates your life. In other words, we each create our own reality. So, if you do not like your life, the first step is simple: change your thinking."

"From what, to what?" Mac asked.

"Just as your meal arrived, I was saying that people think at the rate of several hundred words a minute, depending on the type you are. I was about to say that, unfortunately, most of that thinking is what I term as *trash thoughts*. This does not make a person bad, or wrong, just misguided. We have already established what happens if you think trash thoughts, but I will recap: your thoughts create your focus, and your focus creates your life's reality. So, change your thinking away from what you do not like in you and in your life toward what you do like in you and in your life."

"Suppose you can't think of anything good about yourself and can't find anything good in your life?" Steve asked.

"Then you ask a friend to give you a list of all the good and positive qualities in you as a person," Deliverance replied.

"That's when you find out who your friends are!" Gus joked.

"True enough," Deliverance agreed. "And you do need people around you who can see those qualities. If the people in your life have and express all the negative qualities that you most focus on, then you need to get them out of your life. Ask yourself this: how can you bring change into your life if you are overwhelmed by people who can only offer you more of the same?"

There were several minutes of silence.

Steve shrugged. "I guess you can't."

Deliverance nodded at him. "Thank you. You are right, of course. You cannot make new changes if you are overwhelmed by old programs. And if your friends are the old programs, then they are not truly your friends; they are your handicap."

"That's a bit tough," Steve said.

Deliverance smiled at him. "I take it that this means your friends are the old program?"

Steve nodded again. "They are. Yes."

"So make your choice. New change and new friends, or more of the same with old programs. Which is it to be?"

"New change, and all that it takes to make it happen," Steve said in a clear voice, "but I don't have to like it."

"Then be very sure that it will not happen," Deliverance said gently. "Because if you do not like it, then you will resist. A habit such as yours will be tough enough to break if you have everything on your side, but with you against you, what do you expect the outcome to be?"

"Even I can see the sense of that, Steve," Gus offered.

"Christ! That's a tall order, telling my friends to get lost. I'm damned if I can see how that's going to help me." Steve was feeling increasingly threatened.

"Nobody is suggesting that," Deliverance said patiently. "However, you can tell your friends that you have had enough of the downhill slide in your life and that you will welcome their support in the changes you want to bring into your life. You can outline to them the positive changes that you want and ask for their help. How does that sound?"

Steve sat red-faced and silent.

"They would laugh at you, wouldn't they?" Mike said. "They would think that you're a first-class nut case and that you think that you're too good for them. Right?"

Steve's mouth was a tight, grim line.

"We will continue when you are ready to face this issue," Deliverance said. "Take your time. There is no hurry."

Ten minutes passed while Steve looked ever more glum and threatened. After a few covert glances, Mike, Gus and Mac finished the remains of their meal.

"For the first time in many years, I'm not going to light up a cigar after an excellent meal. From this moment, I quit," Gus said, feeling inspired. He looked proudly at the others.

"Well done," Mike said sincerely. "A good choice."

Steve abruptly began sobbing. For a few moments, deep gut-wrenching sobs tore their way from deep within. He looked at the others from eyes of anguish.

"Yes, they would laugh at me. Every one of them. And it hurts. I've always looked on them as my buddies, but I know that they would mock me and ridicule me. I've known for a long time that what I call a shit-house life, they consider to be normal."

"And there is the difference," Deliverance said softly.

"Are they wrong?" Gus asked. "Maybe, if life seems empty and hostile all the time, that becomes normality. Maybe it's better to adapt to that, and survive, than continually frustrate yourself by wanting something better." He struggled. "It's just a thought. But there's a hell of a lot of people around like that."

"But you never accepted it as normal," Deliverance said, "and it's because of that, that you will be able to move on to a more positive, uplifting life. If you do not dream of better things, a more positive way, how can you expect to reach it? Even then, dreams are not enough. To reach the dreams, we are required to live them. Tell me, how do you see it Steve?"

"I see two sides of it," Steve said shakily. "Shit! I've lived in it long enough. My mates were never as miserable and morose as me. They dealt with life as it came to them and blamed other people — the government, the police, anybody — for their misfortunes. I could never quite see it that way. And, by God, I tried. I succeeded in getting angry at the government, but I could never get rid of the feeling that it was me who screwed up my life, not the government or other people. Mind you, the bloody fat-cat government has a lot to answer for. Anyway, what it all boils down to is simple, and I intend to move on."

"What will you do?" Mac asked.

"I'm bloody well going to move. I'm going to leave all my

mates behind and I'm going to move to another part of the city. I don't know how I'm going to do that on my pathetic income, and it'll probably be a move from one shit-house to another, but I can't just give up. I couldn't live with that at all, and I know perfectly well that I couldn't change their way of seeing life. Hell, I even tried once, and they laughed at me. And why not? What did I have to offer that could really show them that I might be right? That perhaps there is more to life than living up shit-house creek!"

"Even though you could not offer them, or you, the way to bring about change, you spoke from your intuitive knowing of Truth," Deliverance said. "It was a classic case of Truth out of timing. However, the fact that you could never relinquish that Truth has created the timing. That is why you are here, now. This is your opportunity to learn how to create and implement the changes that you want to bring into your life, an opportunity that you have created."

"It's going to be tough," Steve said reflectively.

Deliverance smiled at him. "If tough is your belief and focus, you will, of course, be right."

"Suppose I said that I can do it easily. Would that come true?" Steve asked.

"If you focus on, and believe, that it can be and will be easy to bring positive, uplifting change into your life, then that is the reality that you will create."

"Gee! That would be a change in itself," Steve said.

"I can give you a good starting point," Deliverance offered. "Never again use the word 'shit-house.' Not about you, your life, a situation, or other people. Every time you use that word you empower it, and because it comes from you, it is you who receives the benefit of its creation. For you it is a repetitive word, creating a repetitive reality."

Steve grinned. "Yeah, it's a shit-house word! But, I do hear what you're saying and I'll try not to use it anymore."

"Let me give you another angle on repetition that you may understand more easily," Deliverance said, "and the angle is sameness."

"Sameness!" Gus echoed.

Deliverance nodded. "You got it. Sameness is a killer, and the one enemy that it most tries to destroy is change. When sameness and change occupy a person simultaneously, invariably there is inner conflict. Listen carefully and let this sink in. You cannot change and remain the same. Think about that."

"You cannot change and remain the same," Mike repeated slowly. "Hey, I like that. It's so obvious, but so overlooked. We all want certain changes in our life and we even invite them; but, when they arrive, we nearly always resist them. It doesn't make sense, but that's what we do. Is that why? Is it because we want to change and remain the same?

Deliverance nodded. "It is a subconscious program. Part of the confusion of life for most people."

"But why?" asked Gus. "I mean, I can see it clearly in my own life, but I'm buggared if I know why I resist."

"It is simple enough," Deliverance began. "People are very good at enduring and living with their discord, their inner confusion, their indecision, their apathy, their wanting and never having, their second-rate lives, their poverty, their inability to cope, their drugs, both prescribed and illegal. These are just mere glimpses of what so many people endure. And, I must add, these are not just problems for low-income people. Those with financial wealth often have to endure the erosion of their personal integrity, the pettiness of business, the ruthlessness, the back-stabbing, the sordid affairs, the loss of personal esteem and self-worth as they become part of a corrupt team just for financial gain or for the fear of financial loss. However, it is also a fact that most of the people involved would deny that what I have just listed is a part of their lives. They see only what their program allows them to see."

"That's scary," Gus said.

"True, but this is the way of it, and so it continues, with people in all walks of life addicted to the degrees of suffering that they create and endure. Odd as it may seem, that multilayered suffering becomes so commonplace, so absolutely normal, that it is habitually repeated from one life frame to another." He looked at the others. "Are you with me?"

They all nodded vigourously.

"When inner suffering and discord become so normal, acceptable, and expected, to the extent that a Prime Minister can make a statement to the effect that *'life was not meant to be easy,'* then you find that the addictive nature of humanity has accepted lives and life-styles far below their potential. That is, below both their material and spiritual potential. Within this framework, apathy is given birth, grows rapidly, and dominates most of society. We accept our stagnant sameness as normal; it is our lot.

"Imagine now, a dynamic catalyst is thrown in, and the name of this catalyst is *change*. Can you see it being welcomed with open arms and embraced? The reality is that the conditioned program of the masses sternly resists. In other words, the prison that holds people is called *sameness*, while the key to open the prison is *change*. Sameness fights to keep the door closed, change struggles to open it. Sameness has a conditioned subconscious program to help it resist. Change has the power of newness, the source of its dynamic energy. By stripping all this to its most basic levels, the struggle is between sameness and change, the old and the new. Together they will always be, for the nature of humanity is such that we contain both.

"The art of living is to maintain both in a dynamic and balanced explosion of life energy, which simultaneously allows established and proven foundations of the past to remain, while building on them with the bricks of creativity born in this moment. This is the way of nature, of natural life. This is the way that the successes of the past can be married to the new creativity of the moment. In this way, the old and the new, from their coexistence, create a dynamic that is nameless and ageless. It is a spiritual movement in humanity; a movement into which we are continually born anew, in each moment. I call this *the movement in the moment*. It is the place of life, the only place of true reality."

Mike, Gus, Steve and Mac sat staring at Deliverance, listening as though mesmerised. When Deliverance stopped speaking, the silence was vibrant.

"Wow!" Mike exclaimed.

"Wow, indeed," Deliverance said, smiling at them fondly.

"Can people actually live like this?" Steve asked.

"Of course. How could it be Truth if it was never to be expressed in humanity? I have given you just a glimpse of your potential. This is the way that I live, and be assured, there are many more like me."

"Is this why you seem in such control all the time?" asked Gus. "It seems so very dominant in you."

"It only seems that I am in control, or dominant, because your life is such a continuous, uncertain, powerless wobble. Would a surfboard rider seek to control the wave or would he or she seek Oneness with the wave? I suggest that the wave rider attempts no control at all, but finds the greatest joy and expression of creativity in riding the crest of the wave as it grows, powerfully unfolds, and meets its eventual destruction."

"That's a beautiful model for life," Mike said.

Deliverance waved his hand high, and moments later the waiter came, removed their plates, and presented them with the desert menu.

Gus, Steve and Mac quickly decided on a powerhouse in taste named *Death by Chocolate*, while Mike chose a simple, homemade macadamia-and-cherry ice cream.

Deliverance stayed silent, giving the others time to begin the digestion of what he had said. And, by the pensive looks on their faces, that was exactly what was happening.

CHAPTER SEVEN

A MODEL FOR LIVING

"You can take that as a model for living, as Mike so beautifully described it, and make it your way of life," Deliverance said.

"But what about the magic formula?" Steve asked. "Do we get to use it soon?"

"Are you looking for an easy way out?"

"I suppose so. Isn't that natural?" Steve replied.

"The sooner you realize that there is no quick fix, the sooner you will be able to come to terms with your reality. You created the mess that you are in, and it took a lot of time and effort. Is it not reasonable that some time and effort are required to bring about change?" Deliverance asked.

"I suppose so," Steve said reluctantly.

"The magic formula has its own perfect timing, and that is when I will share it with you. If you have a formula that produces results, but you have no idea why the formula works or any of the principles involved, then you become dependent either on the formula or on the person who gave it to you. How different is that from any other addiction?"

Deliverance gazed around the table. "So far, I have been generalising about life, but soon we will look at your individual lives, one at a time. You probably do not yet realize it, but what you each are attempting to achieve is balance. Nothing more, nothing less. Be aware that balance does not mean being fixed in a mode of living that seems comfortable and safe. Balance is a dynamic, light, very alive way of living, continually embracing the new. Balance and imbalance move in and out of a dynamic juxtaposition in a continual dance. Balance is a response to life rather than a reaction."

Mike was nodding his head in agreement when Mac spoke.

"You'll need to explain that last bit to me. If this is new age stuff, it's not so much totally new to me as very unfamiliar."

"I am happy to explain it, but why would you call wisdom and insight new age? Is it that we live in a time of such vast ignorance that to be wise and enlightened is something new? Wisdom and enlightenment are far older than humanity," Deliverance replied. "However, I take it you need further explanation about balance?"

Mac nodded.

"In any moment of our life," Deliverance continued, "when we suddenly are confronted by an unexpected situation or by something that has just been said to us, we either react or respond. Each is very different. Reaction is fear-based, a repetitive conditioning from the past. In other words, to react is repeating an old action. Remember what I just told you about sameness? Well, reaction and repetition are lovers! From their alliance they give birth to sameness. To respond means that we come from the moment in newness. Love responds, while fear reacts. Old programs are wiped if we learn to respond to life's challenges, whereas reaction simply reinforces them. Is that clear?"

"It never ceases to amaze me that such seemingly insignificant actions can deliver such huge rewards," Mike said wondering. "I've seen the differences between response and reaction before and I've really tried to bring them into my own life. The results are very positive and powerful, but it's not very easy to do."

Gus looked puzzled. "Why not? It sounds easy enough."

"What would you know, you fat freak!" Mike snapped.

"Up yours, you ignorant bastard," Gus shouted, jumping to his feet, his fists clenched.

Mike smiled at him. "You see what I mean?"

His jaw dropping, Gus flopped heavily into his chair. "Oh, Christ!" For moments he sat shaking his head. "Well, you showed me that clear enough. I'm sorry."

"I rest my case," Mike replied.

"Not every trigger is as obvious as an insult."

With a broad smile, Deliverance held out his arms in a wide gesture, and with a sense of shock Mike felt embraced. It felt as though physical arms gently held him, and startled, he glanced at the others. Steve also had a surprised look on his face, while Mac was frowning uncertainly as he, too, looked at the others. Only Gus seemed oblivious to anything odd.

Slowly, very slowly, his eyes closed, Deliverance brought his arms closer to his chest as though he was intently hugging some invisible person.

Mike's face now registered astonishment, but he gave himself easily to the sensation of a huge, gentle hug. Steve's eyebrows were climbing up his forehead, his body tense, but gradually he relaxed, a peaceful expression coming over his face. Mac's face registered panic, and he struggled against nothing as he tried, and failed, to lift his arms. Sweat broke out on his face, and he moaned in fear.

Gus stared at him in astonishment, then looked at each of the others. "What in the hell is wrong with all of you?"

"You mean you can't feel anything?" Mike asked him.

"Why should I? What is there to feel?" Gus replied.

Mike looked toward Deliverance as the man lowered his arms, freeing each of them from their personal experience. "I felt your arms around me," Mike said to him, "and it was wonderful, but I would like an explanation. How do you do such a thing?"

"I held you in my consciousness, but gently, not in any way imprisoned. Gus felt nothing, for it was too foreign an experience to register in him. Steve felt a moment of fear, then he relaxed into it. Mac reacted so powerfully that he froze, and it was his own shutdown reaction that imprisoned him. In other words, Mike and Steve both responded to the moment, but Mac reacted. In him, the flight-fight-or-freeze syndrome was triggered, and he froze. Only moments earlier, Gus jumped into the fight mode. Now, be honest, boys, did either of you consciously choose fight and freeze?"

Gus shook his head ruefully. "No choice here. I was shouting insults and ready to fight in an instant's reaction."

Mac grinned lamely. "Christ, you have to admit it was weird. But I just froze up, there was no choice involved."

Deliverance looked at the other two. "And you, Mike?"

"Well, I felt lightly embraced, didn't understand, but I responded to my feelings of being nurtured," Mike explained.

"That nearly says it for me," Steve agreed, "but I did react at first and began to tense up. Then I felt ... er, well, loved, and I was able to relax." He looked a bit sheepish.

"So, there we have it. A full spectrum of results to one small, nonphysical act," said Deliverance. "Two made a choice and two abdicated from that privilege. Consider, then, that our inner buttons constantly are being pushed daily in our normal lives. Every reaction means that particular button will be re-pushed. Then the results are reenacted and replayed in your lives."

He briefly closed his eyes.

"And they wonder why history constantly repeats itself," he murmured. "Every time you respond to a challenging situation or person, you are leaving old habits and repetitive conditioning behind. You are detaching yourself from the past and moving on. Which of these two ways of living — reaction or response —

do you think is going to offer you the most creative and supportive life-style?"

"Well, it's obvious isn't it?" Gus stated.

"Of course. But you have to agree with Mike. It is not particularly easy. You are required to bring your focus into the moment, the place of life. Do you think that you can do this?"

Gus shrugged. "I can but try."

Deliverance smiled at him. "I can ask for nothing more, but I would like it if that statement was made with power and enthusiasm. What are your feelings, Gus? Are they casual and could not care less, or something more positive?"

"I take your point," Gus nodded. "It's so easy to get into a slack attitude at work and at home. I think perhaps it's a defense mechanism I use to avoid being derided. Odd as it seems, I was an enthusiastic kid who constantly got jeered at because of my positive, gung-ho manner. So I withdrew it. To be honest, even I don't like the way I sound nowadays."

"Remember, Gus, that we become the thoughts we speak aloud and we become our attitudes. A person with angry thoughts is an angry person. A person with a slack attitude is a slack person. We can all see that in other people, but so few of us can see it in ourselves. People have the strange idea that what we see in other people does not apply to ourselves."

Deliverance looked at Gus thoughtfully, "I think that you are ready for this. You are very overweight, as you well know. Looking at your body, I know immediately that you are a very defensive person. You have inadvertently built that defense into your physical body to shield the sensitive soul within."

"Fancy that. And I thought it was because I eat too much," Gus said in a droll, hurt voice.

Deliverance smiled at him. "Oh, you do. You eat far too much of all the wrong food, but there is a reason. You are an emotional eater. You eat to feed the ravenous appetite of your suppressed and denied emotions. Unfortunately, they can never be satisfied by food. Dampened, but not satisfied. Be honest now. You have just had a large, satisfying meal, and your stomach is full. But you are still hungry. Yes?"

Gus sighed deeply. "Yep! I was wondering if there are any snacks on offer. I'm full and I feel hungry. But why?"

"When you were a little boy and you ran to mummy crying, hurt or upset, how did she comfort you? Was it with hugs and kisses and a lot of love? Or was it with sweets and biscuits, and very little of the true closeness from your mother that you craved?"

Blinking furiously, Gus looked away. He breathed heavily for a while before attempting an answer. "It's pretty obvious by my reaction, isn't it? Sweets and biscuits, of course. And all I ever really wanted was a hug to know that I was loved." He sighed again. "And I'm still wanting, aren't I?"

"Didn't Harriet ever give you the love you craved?" Mike asked. "She seemed to be outgoing and expressive."

"Yeah, in the early days. But I could never get enough of her affection. I'm not talking sex here. I'm talking affection, of touching, holding hands in the street, kissing when we meet. All that stuff." He sighed again. "I long ago realized that Harriet was like Mum. She just doesn't have it in her."

"My dear friend," Deliverance said gently, "unlikely as it seems, Harriet is offering you the greatest gift that you could possibly receive in this lifetime, but you do not recognize it."

Gus stared at him, stunned, then shook his head sadly. "You just lost me completely. I've no idea what you mean."

"You have a need for affection from a person you love," Deliverance explained, "and without it you become defensive and emotionally withdrawn. Even to you, this must communicate certain messages. You have developed dependencies on other people for your sense of well-being. In some past life you lost touch with self-worth: the inner reliance that simply knows you are a splendid and worthwhile person, no matter what the issue or what others may think. Perhaps as the result of some disastrous love affair or even some deep and violent row with your mother, in that past life you became emotionally flawed. In view of what you said to Mike when you reacted to him, I suspect that you were illegitimate, a bastard, with deep needs for a woman's love. It is obvious that the dependency is placed in the opposite sex.

"You developed an emotional need to be constantly reassured. In this present life, you drew your mother to you because she would not reinforce that need. You married Harriet because on a soul level you knew that she, also, would not reinforce that need. On a deeper level, you know that the last thing that you need is a person who will cultivate and maintain that emotional dependency. In this life, you elected to heal your inner emotional imbalance. Unbeknown to you, to your mother or to your wife, you all elected on a soul level to play the roles that would make you face this issue and resolve it for all time. That, my friend, is the nature of their gift."

Gus sat goggle-eyed. "My God!"

Deliverance chuckled. "Your God, indeed." He looked at Gus keenly. "Take your time and feel into what I have said. And I do mean feel into it. Your intellect and thoughts will be working overtime, but I want you to also feel from the heart. So, when you are ready, let me know if you can relate to what I have said."

For ten minutes Gus had a hurt, sad, faraway look on his chubby, ageing face. The others ordered coffee for themselves and for him, while thinking about what Deliverance had said. They knew in their hearts that, on different levels, what he had said also applied to them.

Finally, Gus sighed. "Yeah, I have to admit that it makes sense. I have to tell you, though, that until now if anyone had told me this, I would have said they were crazy."

He stared hard at Deliverance. "You have an ability, and energy, that somehow strips away all the garbage so that a person is faced with glaringly obvious truth. What is so strange is that all my life it was hidden, with not a clue about what you said. Then, wham! My nose is right up against it and, from some place so deep inside that I did not even know it existed, I clearly recognize what you are telling me." He shook his head in wonder. "Man, this is weird. If Mike had told me a few days ago that all this would be happening to me now, I would have recommended him for psychiatric treatment. Now, I have to look at possibilities that I didn't know were even possible!"

"You handled it well, Gus," Deliverance said with a smile. "The reason you are able to recognize the truth of what I am saying is simply timing. Despite your lack of awareness, you have created both the timing and the opportunity to be exposed to your own truth. Now, the question is, what are you going to do with it?"

Gus shook his head. "I'm a bit confused about that right now, but I guess ... er ... I'm definitely going to have to do something to deal with it. What would you suggest?"

"I suggest that you withdraw your emotional need that is based in your wife and daughters and decide whether or not you like yourself, or even if you are able to like yourself. Think about that tomorrow and be clear about it. We will base our focus in your life for now and give you an opportunity to resolve this emotional problem. And remember, a problem is an opportunity waiting to be recognized and acted upon."

Gus looked pensive, gazing at the ceiling for long moments. "I don't think I like myself at all, but I'm pretty damn sure that I can. Already I can feel circuits of understanding making inner connections, and I feel something I long ago lost. I feel hope. I don't need a day to think this over. I remember when I was a kid I thought that I was something pretty damn special. And that didn't go down well at all. I got jeered at and put down so much ... I came to believe the opposite."

He glared at Mike and the others. "And none of you helped. You all did your share of trying to make me feel small."

"Is that what you feel people were doing to you, making you feel small?" Deliverance asked.

"Yeah. That's what it felt like, anyway."

"And your mother and wife?" Deliverance prompted.

"Yeah, them as well. Mum didn't when I was a little kid, but as I grew older she did. Same with Harriet. When we first met she was loving and supportive. But, after we got married, she began to make me feel small, as though I was incapable or something. And it just got worse."

"And then you got really serious about overeating?"

Gus grinned. "Yeah, that's for sure."

"Do you see," Deliverance asked, "that you began to eat to get larger? You felt that people made you small — your own words — and that life was reducing you. So, on a subconscious level, you attempted to get bigger to prove them wrong. By eating and making your body bigger, you attempted to deny them and their words, but all it did was exacerbate the problem. And all this reactionary behaviour not only eluded your awareness, but it also eroded your inner confidence, making you even more dependent on the affection and approval of those you love."

"Yeah," Gus said dourly. "Approval-seeking is involved as well. If they weren't affectionate, then they didn't approve. And if they didn't approve, they sure as hell didn't love me. God, it all seems so clear now. Embarrassingly clear."

"You needn't be embarrassed, Gus," Mike said. "There are millions of people like you, and they don't yet know it. You do. So this is the time and place to begin the changes."

"I tell you, this might not be my immediate problem, but I've just learned a hell of a lot about myself," Steve said.

"Yes," Mac said seriously. "Me, too."

"So what do I do with all this ... mess?" Gus asked.

"You do realize that you probably chose feeling *small* as a derogatory definition because you were a shortish, slender man. No doubt that you would have liked to be a tall man, so being short made you feel small, inferior," Deliverance said.

"Yeah, that too," Gus agreed.

"What you do, first, is face who you are. Physically, you are now a shortish fat man, but this is not natural. In your natural body, you are a shortish *slim* man. A perfect body for excellent health and well-being. Being tall offers no special advantage in life or life-styles, nor is it more manly. So, first face your natural physique and feel good with it. Accept it. Okay. Emotionally, you are dependent on those you love, even though they offer you nothing to support that dependency. In your natural emotional state, you look within for your well-being, knowing that it can never come from an external source. It can be supported and nourished from an outside source, but not developed or maintained.

"Finally, the intellect. You are, by now, intellectually blocked and convinced that you are inadequate, and this sense of mental inadequacy can affect your work, your intellectual relationship with your family, and your attitude to life. You have developed a defensive and offensive cynicism. In truth, however, you are a naturally bright and perceptive person, quick, and very capable intellectually. Would you agree with this summary?"

Gus nodded, looking embarrassed. "That about sums it up. Sounds like I'm really stuffed."

"Possibly so," Deliverance said with a smile, "but definitely not unstuffable. What you have to do now is make a choice. What I would like you to do is think about it, then at home write and describe in detail the person that you think you should be and would like to be."

Gus looked sceptical. "Are you kidding?"

Deliverance stared him in the eyes, straight and stern.

"Do I look like I am kidding? How do you expect to put your life back in order, into a way that you want it to be, if you are not clear about what that order or want is? If you have only a vague, unformed sense of the self you should be, that vague and unformed self is what you will achieve. If you remember, I told you the other night that we each have a mission in life. Can you remember what that mission is?"

Gus stared at him uncertainly for several minutes, then shook his head in defeat.

"I can tell ... " Mike began, subsiding as Deliverance cut him off.

"Mac, do you remember what that mission is?"

"Yes, er, well, it was something about more of what we, er, or less than ... oh hell, I can't get it."

Deliverance looked at Steve. "Well, I've had a chance to think, but I'm not sure if I've got it right. Our mission," he began slowly, "is to make ... ourselves ... more of ... what we are ... and less of what we ain't," he finished in a rush. He beamed. "I got it, huh?"

"You got it," Deliverance said smiling. "So, Gus. I suggest you pay better attention from now on, because there is nothing wrong with either your brain or memory. If you are going to make yourself more of what you are, then I suggest you become very clear about what you are. Write about it on a physical, emotional and intellectual level."

He looked at his watch. "It's close to midnight, boys, and everyone else has gone home. I think it is your turn now. You have had enough for tonight. Oh, and Gus, tomorrow night I would like you to share with all of us what you have written. Remember, boys, eight o'clock tomorrow night, and dinner is on the house."

CHAPTER EIGHT

CHANGING THE PROGRAMS

Mike smiled to himself when, at ten minutes to eight on the following evening, Gus and Mac walked into The Offbeat Eatery, amiably chatting to each other.

Sitting at the bar, sipping on a grapefruit juice while he waited, Mike mused over the fact that he had yet to see Deliverance eat anything. This did not mean that Deliverance did not eat, he reflected, but if and when he did, it was when Mike was not around.

Moments later, he watched as Steve came bounding in, looking more open and vital than he had in a long time. Gone was the closed down, defensive person that he had become. He now looked more like the Steve that Mike had known in the past.

As the others went over to the table they had shared the previous evening, Mike could not help but notice the greater enthusiasm in the way they greeted each other. He also noted that they all, himself included, carried a folded sheet of paper.

Mike joined them, followed only moments later by a smiling Deliverance. Glancing up at the clock on the opposite wall, Deliverance grinned at each one of them.

"Wonderful. Everybody on time and already with a new, more enthusiastic, life energy. Do you boys feel it?"

"It's startlingly obvious to me," Mike said.

"Yep! I feel like a new man, already," Steve said, "and you haven't even started on me yet."

Gus grinned. "It's a bit more complicated for me. It's as though

I am looking at myself from a slightly different position, and I'm beginning to like what I see."

"I reckon I've got a long way to go," Mac added, "and I sort of dread my turn coming up, yet ... I can't wait. I feel .... hopeful."

"Guess what?" Gus asked. "I saw Pete today. He was in uniform, but we had a quick coffee together. He asked me to apologize to all of you for him. He didn't intend to be so reactive and feels bad about it. I told him that there were no hard feelings, and I asked him if he wanted to join in with our evening sessions. He said, no offense, but it wasn't for him."

Mike felt a sense of relief that all was well. He had not wanted their old friendship to end on such a sour note.

Once again the menu was studied, with Mac and Gus again deciding on steak, this time with French fries. Steve went for lamb with mint sauce and steamed vegetables. Mike chose a Caesar salad. Gus and Steve each had a beer, while Mac and Mike shared a bottle of red. Deliverance had his usual tall glass of grapefruit juice.

Smiling broadly, Deliverance indicated the folded paper they each carried.

"Well done, boys. This shows initiative. It seems that each of you is ready to define what and who it is you are and want to be. So how about we start with you, Gus? Read out to us what you have written."

Gus grinned weakly. "I've been dreading this all day ... and looking forward to it."

Spreading his sheet of paper on the table, he began reading. "Physically, I want to be the slim and fit man that I once was. I want to be quick, sure and capable. I want to be able to look in the mirror and like what I see. Emotionally, I want to lose my dependency on those I love for emotional support. I want to be fully emotionally capable within myself. I want to like, and approve, of myself. Intellectually, I want to be able to come to terms with myself. I want to know that I lack nothing intellectually, and that my social status and financial income in no way reflect an inadequate intellect."

He looked around shyly. "That's about it, really. Not a lot written, but a hell of a lot thought about."

"That says it well, Gus," Deliverance said approvingly. "And you have stated it with the essential clarity."

"I'll go next," said Steve, "if that's okay."

Everyone nodded.

"I did a lot of thinking and self-searching, too," Steve began, "and I didn't like much of what I saw in myself. I looked at myself, clearly, for the first time in a long while. What I found was self-pity. Buckets of it. Wheel barrow loads! I realised that just about everything that I always described as shit was my own self-pity. Physically, I feel okay about myself. A bit soft and overweight, but that's easily fixed. Emotional eating applies to me also. Spot on! I definitely drink too much, but that isn't out of control ... yet! So, I want to be physically fit, that's for sure. I want to be self-supportive within myself. I want to like myself ... hell! ... maybe even love myself. I think this is the most important area for me, to like and accept myself. I want to stop blaming myself for everything that goes wrong and have a more positive relationship with myself and life. And, of course, not last, nor least, I want a good job that pays well, with work that I enjoy." He looked at the others and shrugged. "And I'd like a woman in my life who really loves me."

"Wouldn't we all?" Mac muttered. "I suppose I might as well continue?" he asked, glancing at Deliverance.

"That was admirable, Steve, very clear and certainly achievable." Deliverance said, then he nodded to Mac.

Mac took a deep breath, releasing it slowly. "More than anything, I definitely want a loving woman in my life. And I am very clear about this." He glanced at his sheet of paper. "The other thing I most want is good self-esteem." He looked around. "Like the others here, I want to like myself. That's important. The other thing is, er ... this isn't easy to talk about. It makes me feel ashamed, but it's all connected to my lack of self-esteem."

He looked at Deliverance, embarrassed. "I want to get rid of the almost non-stop sex talk that takes place in my head. Some people might think it's funny. Believe me, it isn't. I want to live without sexual frustration, without loathing myself because of my nasty, dirty thoughts." He was silent a moment, a deep red blush suffusing his face. "And I want to live without the need of wanking. It's all caught up in a tangled web. The sexual thoughts, the burning sexual desire, the awful frustration, and then the wanking. Followed immediately by self-hatred and self-loathing. And I don't know how to end it. I don't know how to stop my dirty sexual thoughts. It all defeats me, utterly, and I hate it."

He sighed heavily. "I love my son, Sam. He's great. But I am terrified of what he would think of me if he knew what a totally useless specimen I really am. I hate my work. I work in a modern university, teaching and coaching, and I hate it." He shook his head. "I'm lost in my own bloody mess. So, if I have to be clear about what I want myself to be, it comes down to one thing: I want to be a person that *I* can be proud of, that *I* can respect, and that *I* can learn to love."

"You do not lack the courage," Deliverance said, looking directly at Mac. "That could not have been easy. And you can have what you want."

They all looked expectantly at Mike.

"Well, mine is very simple." Mike said, folding his slip of paper and sliding it into his hip pocket. "I like myself and my life. I love my wife and children. But I want to build on liking myself into fully loving and accepting myself. I want to be an enlightened person and teach other people like you do." He was looking at Deliverance as he finished speaking.

Deliverance smiled warmly at all of them. "For all of you, what you want, you can have. This is no problem at all. But, you are required to live what you want, not simply want it. Wanting never has, nor ever will, supply what you want. It all has to do with focus. Remember focus? Energy flows where you focus. In other words, your life is made up, and fabricated, from the substance of what it is that you focus on. For Gus, this is an emotional dependency. For Mac, sexual frustration. For Steve, self-pity. For all of you, this means, in effect, that you attract and maintain exactly what it is that you least want in your life. Remember, your mind does not know the difference between what you do want and what you do not want; it only knows what you focus on. And what you focus on, like a magnet, your mind attracts. You boys all suffer from wrong focus. Is this clear? We must be sure that you fully understand what I am saying, otherwise you will be unable to act on it."

"So our focus is on becoming more of what we want to be?" Steve suggested. "As in what we have written?"

"I take it this means that I should not even think about my emotional needs," Gus said. "But what do I think about? My thoughts naturally migrate toward my problems."

"And thus sustains them," Deliverance said. "Have you seen any indication that suggests otherwise?"

"No," Gus said decisively. "It seems that the more I think about it, tormenting myself and reacting, the worse it gets."

"Same here," Mac said heavily.

Nodding, Deliverance said quietly, "The power of focus."

At that moment their waiter appeared at the table, his large tray loaded. Quickly and deftly he placed their plates before them, followed by numerous sauces. Then, wishing them a hearty meal, he departed. "You see?" Deliverance grinned. "You focus on your food, and it arrives. Enjoy."

For long minutes they were too busy eating to talk, but soon, they slowed down.

"By the same token," Deliverance said, "what do you think you would attract if you focused only on hunger?"

"More hunger, reasons to be without food," Mike said. "Gosh! It's like ... you have to rethink everything."

"Of course. That's what I keep trying to show you."

"Can you expand on how we individually handle it?" Steve asked. "I just want to hear it said, so that I'm clear."

"You are finally clear that self-pity attracts more reasons into your life for you to continue pitying yourself?" Deliverance asked. "A destructive, negative, self-created and self-maintained cycle that can, and does, last for lifetimes."

"Yeah. I really get it. If I call everything that goes wrong in my life, shit-house, then it's me creating and maintaining the shit in my house, in me, and in my life. Right?"

"Let me ask how much of your thinking is self-critical?"

"Only about ninety-nine percent," Steve replied.

"And you, boys?" Deliverance asked Mac and Gus.

Mac opened and closed his mouth a couple of times, but no words emerged. Finally, he croaked, "About the same."

Gus grinned, resigned. "About ninety-five percent, I reckon."

"If you remember some of my preamble," Deliverance said with a smile, "I mentioned criticism is one of the most powerful and destructive forces that we can unleash against ourselves. Self-criticism is a savage attack on the physical heart, on the emotional body, and is intellectually self-defeating. Everything you criticise in yourself by your focus, you develop, maintain and enforce. Until it destroys you."

"Did you say an attack on the heart?" Gus asked.

"No. I said a savage attack on the heart. Every time you criticize yourself, it has a similar effect to a hand brutally squeezing your heart. It is a non-sustainable attack."

"I never heard anything like that before," Mac said.

Deliverance laughed aloud. "There is so very much about life that you have never yet heard, my friend. So very much. Even now, we but scratch the surface. It is all about Truth and timing. First, we deal with the itch. Then, maybe, we look at which came first, the itch, or the need to scratch! For now, be very clear that nothing creative will ever come from self-criticism."

"What about a literary or movie critic?" Gus asked.

"You will learn more about the critic than you will learn about the book or movie. But to review it is quite different. A critic begins from a negative base, the reviewer is neutral. The critic who begins from a positive base, looking at how good the item is and how it could be made better, is a constructive critic. That is a positive offering, but it's rare. Self-criticism is almost never based in positives, just the negatives. What we are talking about is self-attack with no possibility of self-defense. Are you clear enough about this?"

"Yeah," Steve sighed. "That's me ... again."

"I have a thousand buts," Gus said, grinning. "But they are all empty. Bubbles of futile protest, based in senseless habit."

"As you make it clear, it all seems so damn obvious," Mac said. "I struggle to believe that I could be so stupid for so long."

"If you think and talk like that, it will be longer yet. You are doing it again. Wrong focus. Forget stupid. Let stupid go. You need a better focus. So give me one ... now!" Deliverance said sharply.

"I'm amazed at how I could be misinformed for so long, and that I could continue that way. Especially when I realize how intelligent and resourceful I am," Mac said, with a shy, embarrassed look on his face.

"Yes! Yes! You've got it!" Mike whooped. "Tell me, Mac, which feels better, stupid or intelligent?"

"Okay, smart-arse, I get it," Mac grinned.

"Right, boys," Deliverance said, "I think the message has been received. Criticism does not work in your best interest. So what we have to decide is, what will?"

"How about self-appreciation?" Mike asked.

"Deliverance smiled. "How does that feel with you boys? Do you think that you could replace self-criticism with self-appreciation?"

"I don't see why not," Steve said seriously. "I mean, it would have to be better, wouldn't it? I can't remember the last time I thought about appreciating myself or anything in my life. Yeah! I reckon Mike's right. Anyway, appreciation must be the opposite of criticism, so it's got to be good."

Deliverance looked at Gus and Mac.

Gus nodded. "I can't think of anything better. So if there's a trick to all this, then I'm tricked. I go for self-appreciation."

"Me too," Mac nodded, "but I don't really understand. Am I supposed to appreciate the brilliance of my sexual thoughts, or applaud the creativity of my dirty mind, or what?"

"Basically, what!" Mike laughed.

As Deliverance shook his head with a smile, the waiter quickly cleared away their plates. Almost immediately, another waiter appeared with a tray of dessert.

"Thought I would choose dessert for you tonight, boys. I think that you will enjoy it. It's baked apple soaked in rum. An unusual combination that works very well. You may wish to add a touch of honey, maybe not."

He watched as they each tasted the dessert, smiling at their expressions.

"Tell me, Mac, what do you like and enjoy in your life that

you feel you could take credit for?"

Mac looked thoughtful. "I'm ashamed to say it, but that's not an easy question. I like to think that some of the credit for Sam being such a balanced, all-round nice guy, is mine. But mostly, that's his achievement." He stared at them for a while, looking ever more serious. "Christ! Right now, I can't think of anything in my life that I enjoy that I can take credit for. I don't like my thoughts. I don't like my professional life. I don't like my relationships with women." His eyes wide and sad, he stared at Deliverance solemnly. "I can't think of a damn thing."

"That is a sad story," Deliverance said, "Most people can think of a few things in their lives that they enjoy, with all thanks to them. However, we can improvise. Tell me about your potential. Do you have a worthwhile potential, or is it zero?"

Mac roused himself from his gloom. "Ah, that sounds better. Before meeting you, I would have said that my potential was no better than more of the same. But now? I now feel that my potential has expanded greatly. If I can implement all that you have talked about into my life, my potential has moved from zero to exciting."

"If you were to quit your job, what would you do?" asked Deliverance.

Mac smiled. "I know that this sounds stupid — even though I'm not stupid — but I would join a Wilderness Tracking and Field Tour Group, if I could. I've always had the feeling that I would love to be a professional guide. As a hobby, I love it. It's the only thing that keeps me sane."

Deliverance nodded thoughtfully. "That's excellent. So what is stopping you from quitting a job you hate and entering into one that you love?"

Mac looked astonished. "My God! What about all my years of study? All the years I slogged away until I got my qualifications. And then there's the money. I'm well paid, now. God only knows how much, or how little I'd get as a tour guide. I've spent twenty years getting into my present position. Besides, what would all my colleagues think?"

"So the answer is ... fear." Deliverance replied.

"Fear? What do you mean, fear? I never mentioned fear. I gave you my reasons for not quitting," Mac said belligerently.

Deliverance sighed. "Your years of study and your admirable qualifications add up to status and security. You cannot release them, so you are anchored. What anchors you? Fear! You are highly paid in a job you say that you hate, inadvertently maintaining a hate that you cannot separate from yourself. Why? Because money is your security, and you are afraid to let go of security. Why? Fear! And you worry about what your colleagues might think. Why? Fear! Fear that they might think that you are a failure. Fear of their disapproval. Many little fears that add up to you living your life in a prison, and the name of the prison is fear."

"I don't agree with you," Mac said aggressively.

"Now fear is making you aggressive," Deliverance added.

Gus, Steve and Mike avoided looking at Mac, giving him time to sort things out in his mind. They each focused on finishing their baked rum apple while it was still hot.

"Coffee, boys?" Deliverance asked. "We are going to close all further discussion tonight. I will leave you to enjoy your coffee and to chat among yourselves. Mac, I want you to think about what I have put before you. If you cannot see the source of your own fear, then there is no room for change. Fear will always cancel out change. The main pastime of sameness is to create more fear, because fear will defend and maintain sameness. Think about it. I'll see you all tomorrow night at eight o'clock."

CHAPTER NINE

BUILDING THE NEW

Mike kept himself busy the next day doing far more than Deliverance asked of him. Having made friends with the two chefs, he was allowed to watch and learn, plus he helped by washing the numerous kitchen utensils when required.

He also discovered that Deliverance lived in a spacious wing of the restaurant, that behind the wing there was a large garden, and it wasn't just any garden. This was a skilfully created environment of colorful flowering shrubs and trees, and as Mike walked along the enchanting winding paths — discovering nooks and crannies of sculptures and bamboo with a small pond and fountain — he realized that there were varieties of shrubs chosen to flower in every month of the year. It was striking sanctuary in continuous bloom.

That evening, Steve was first through the door, with the others no more than five minutes behind. All were seated at the table by ten minutes to eight.

"I'll get the drinks if you tell me what you want," Mike offered.

"What's it like working for Deliverance?" Steve asked.

"Very quiet and smooth. I don't see much of him. I get the feeling that he has a lot of correspondence," Mike said.

He went and collected their drinks, arriving back at the same time as Deliverance.

"Good evening, boys," he greeted them. Then, without any

small talk, he looked at Mac. "Well, Mac, what has your day's cogitation produced?"

Mac smiled wryly. "A lot. I even took a day off work because I had the feeling that something momentous and important is taking place, and I didn't want to screw up." He stared at Deliverance.

"You do know how to push buttons, don't you? I pondered long and deep about why I stay with my work, and it all made good economic sense. But when I put fear into the equation, I could see the way that I justified my life. I could see that a risk was more frightening for me than more of the same. But something has changed. Now, after many hours of deliberation, I can see that the thought of staying the same is far more frightening than taking a risk. When I think about my life from a freedom angle, it seems dumbfoundingly crazy to stay with a job that I hate. A job that is wrecking my life, my self-esteem and all my potential relationships with women. And, would you believe, I've finally realized that I look to women for salvation through sex. My God! The very idea is absurd, even abhorrent to me, yet this is what I have inadvertently been doing for more years than I care to think about. Even worse, as I ruin each potential relationship, all that is left are the fantasies in the head. Sexual fantasies like I had as a teenager. Dirty and degrading stuff. Then comes the sexual frustration ... and you know what follows that! And last is the self-disgust, especially in knowing that I will keep on repeating this same degrading pattern. It's been downhill all the way. What's worse is the thought of where will it all lead to. The final irony is that I worry about what my peers might think of me if they ever found out, or even worse, if Sam found out. It all sounds pathetic."

"You realize, of course, that what they, or anyone, thinks of you has absolutely no affect on your life unless you take their opinions and create the effect. It is what you think that affects your life. So, Mac. You appear to have done some very effective soul searching. The question is, are you going to do anything with it?" Deliverance asked.

"Yes. I'm going to quit my job."

Gus gasped, while Steve's eyebrows climbed.

"Why?" Deliverance asked.

"What do you mean, why? You as good as suggested it," Mac snapped impatiently.

Deliverance looked at him calmly. "Please answer why. But first, place your order for dinner. And while the boys order, think it over constructively, without reacting."

Mac chose fish, French fries and salad, while Mike again chose a Caesar salad. Both Gus and Steve chose to have apricot chicken with mashed, creamed potatoes and lightly steamed asparagus.

Apart from small talk, nobody said much for nearly fifteen minutes, while Mac stared aggressively into space. Mike was surprised that he had not jumped up and walked out.

Their meals arrived, and apart from Mac, whose mind was not on his food, the others tucked in heartily.

"I'm quitting because my life is on the line," Mac finally said. I'm not entirely stupid." His eyes bulged as he realized what he had said. "Oh God! I didn't mean it like that. Because I am basically intelligent — even though I seldom use it — I can see that the way my life is heading I will soon be dealing with stress-related illness, heart condition, health problems. It's obvious. I'm unhappy, unfulfilled and a victim of my own apathy. In fact, I honestly don't think I have a choice. Apart from other comparatively minor reasons, that's why."

"That was not so difficult to say," Deliverance said. "They are very good reasons for change. I suppose it did occur to you that if you are happy and fulfilled in your work, you will not be looking to women to fill in the empty spaces of your life and your psyche."

Mac nodded. "Yes, it did. But ... I know me ... and I don't think it will change my habitual sexual pattern of thoughts."

Deliverance looked at the others. "Do any of you boys have persistent and habitual thought patterns that dominate your thinking, reducing the quality of your life?"

"Yeah," said Steve. "I do. I have a pattern of slipping into thoughts of self-pity. You know, the *poor me, life is out to get me* type of thoughts. The next step is to blame myself for being so helpless and apathetic. Then I wallow in even more self-pity. A vicious cycle."

"Do you have any hobby or something that you really love to do?" asked Deliverance.

"I love reading," Steve replied. "Sci-fi mostly. And I really enjoy listening to some of the new age music."

Deliverance looked at Gus. "How about you? Do you have any constant thought patterns that help to defeat you?"

Gus looked shamefaced. "Unfortunately, yes. I have this odd little habit of fantasizing scenes where other people depend on me for their emotional well-being. For instance, I fantasize on Harriet or the girls needing my approval for any number of things. And I usually withhold my approval so that they can get a taste of what it feels like. All in all, bloody pathetic."

"And do you have a recreational hobby or something that gives you great pleasure?" Deliverance asked.

Gus laughed. "You might not believe it, but I love to write poetry. It's generally pretty sad stuff, but it's where my feelings can get expressed and my pain laid bare."

Deliverance glanced at Mike. "I take it that you are happy enough with your thoughts?"

"Generally, yes," Mike nodded, "but there's always room for

improvement. However, I'm careful to avoid negative and self-destructive ways of thinking."

"All right, boys, you are going to have to change those thought patterns, and here is how we will do it. First ..."

"Is this the magic formula?" Steve cut in.

Deliverance shook his head slowly. "Not yet, son, but we are beginning to close in on it. Before I give you the formula, you have to show me that you are making progress. Life is not about words from the intellect, it is about action based in intelligence. Sitting here each evening, we are dealing with words and intellect. Naturally, they have their place and timing.

"But our dialogue must be the forerunner to action. In other words, the dialogue needs to be lived. When it is lived it becomes experienced, and experience invariably precipitates us toward change. Of course, change is not automatic. You have to be open to change, or at the very least, it helps. Change is a catalyst in life that is ever present. Change may enter your life at any moment and blow it apart. Generally, people resist change. They prefer more of the same, even while hating it. Our resistance to change generally can be measured by the degree of our daily suffering — and there are many levels and forms of suffering. The more we resist the constant push of change, the more we suffer. Openness, and a willingness to go along with change no matter what it demands, is rare."

He paused to take a sip of grapefruit juice. "However, I am getting off the track. I am going to teach you boys a way of bringing your thoughts into a much better focus that honors you rather than negates and dismisses you. As you no doubt know, the more you oppose your thoughts, the more strongly they oppose you. This is because wrong focus literally creates and feeds opposing energy."

He looked at their plates. "You have finished your main meal, so we will do this now. You can have your desserts later. I warn you, doing this after an evening meal is not good timing, so you will need to stay awake. Please, come with me."

As Deliverance stood up and left the table, the others followed. He led them into his own wing of the large building, and entering a lounge room, indicated that they sit wherever they preferred.

"I want you to sit with your spines as straight as possible," Deliverance said. "Energy flows through a straight spine in a way that is more harmonious to the spirit, making it easier to focus. And you are less inclined to sleep."

Gus and Mac, who each had chosen large armchairs in which to sprawl, sat up quickly. While Gus hauled himself up as straight as possible, Mac chose to sit on the floor, his legs out in front of him, the armchair supporting his back. Mike and Steve had chosen smaller, more upright chairs.

Standing before them so that he could make easy eye contact, Deliverance spoke to them. "Listen carefully, boys, because this is about you and your life. Each of ... "

"Do you just mean us, or anyone?" Steve interjected.

Deliverance frowned at him. "Of course it means anyone, but right now I am talking to you, so pay attention. A human Being has many bodies apart from the physical body. You are unable to physically see the other bodies. They are known as the subtle bodies. Just briefly, they are the emotional body, the mental body, the astral and etheric bodies, and others. More, in fact, than are generally realized. Right now, none of this matters other than that you are aware of it. However, it matters that you know about your Light body. You could call this body the metaphysical self, metaphysical meaning beyond the physical. We all are familiar with our physical bodies, even though the average person's knowledge of his body and its fundamental requirements is nothing short of appalling. However, very few people are familiar with their Light bodies. Now boys, listen carefully. Life is not a physical reality! Life is a spiritual reality of which we have a physical experience. Can you even imagine how limited the unaware person's experience of life really is?"

He looked them in the eyes, one man at a time.

Numbly, they each shook their heads.

"If life is limited to no more than the physical experience of it, then that person's life is very limited. Be aware that, although the physical is the clothing of spirit, our awareness and focus determine our experience of reality. Whether we live in a limited consensus reality, or a limitless greater reality, is entirely up to us. And neither is right or wrong, or good or bad. It is all about choosing.

"We each have a Light body. If we did not, then we could not have a physical body. Our Light body has a far more direct relationship with spirit than our physical body; that is, unless you are extremely aware and spiritually experienced. What I am going to teach you is how to get your focus into your Light body and expand on your experience of life. Not only that, all habitual patterns of destructive behaviour are created on a physical level, but they are carried from one life to another on a metaphysical level. I am going to teach you how to access this and change the patterns by changing the focus. And although it needs a little practice, it is very easy to do!

"Right boys, I want you to relax. I know that Mike has done plenty of this inner work before, but you others are new to it. Be aware that what you are going to do is not really a meditation, it is an inner exercise. Meditation generally is about silence and stillness within, but you are going to be active. You are going to exercise a part of you that has been unused for a long time: your Light body. This exercise requires you to use imagination. I want you to imagine what I will be speaking and become a part of the action. Do not watch it on the screen of your mind as a passive onlooker, be involved. You are a player in this, not a viewer. A participant, not an onlooker. Understand?"

He smiled as the others solemnly nodded.

"All you have to do is follow my instructions and keep your mind with my words. I will speak slowly, with many pauses. Now, before we start, are there any questions?"

"Do you mean that in this inner exercise we will actually see from, and experience from, our Light body?" Steve asked.

Deliverance nodded. "Yes, but the degree of that experience will vary. Do any of you remember how long it took you to learn to physically walk, from when you began to try?"

Looking mystified, the others shook their heads.

"Exactly," Deliverance grinned. "You just know that it took a while, but walking was inevitable if you were physically capable. So, too, with this. In each physical life you again learn to walk, but it takes a while. To focus into life through your Light body, and to experience your Light body, is easier and more natural than walking. It is a bit like an unused muscle. If you use it regularly and give it plenty of exercise, it will get strong and efficient. So, too with your Light body. You receive in the direct proportion to which you invest. In this case, you are investing in self.

"One last thing before we get started. I am going to guide each of you into your Light body, and eventually down a flight of steps. At this point you will each need to go into your own unique experience. So let's look at this. Gus has an emotional dependency, but he loves to create poetry. So for Gus, I recommend that at the bottom of the steps he visualizes and sees a beautiful garden with a summerhouse tucked away beneath some trees on the edge of a pond. Does this appeal, Gus, or would you prefer something different?"

Gus grinned. "It sounds wonderful. But to create my poetry, I prefer to be in a well-appointed coffee house with the right ambience, in the middle of a busy shopping plaza."

Deliverance laughed. "So be it. That is your scene, and that coffee shop is your particular place. Create it, and appoint the coffee shop so it fits comfortably. The main point for each of you is that you create a place that attracts you, so that you want to go back to it on a regular basis."

"I'll take the beautiful garden with the summerhouse," Steve said. "And if it's okay, I'll set it up with a stereo system and a library of my favourite sci-fi books."

"Perfect," said Deliverance, lightly clapping his hands.

"How about you, Mac?"

Mac looked puzzled. "To be honest, I'm not sure."

"How about trekking in the wilderness?" Mike suggested. "It could even be in places that you have never yet visited, so you could allow your imagination freedom to create and even see unknown areas. Imagine all the interaction with nature that you could create."

Mac glanced at him, his eyes bright. "Now that, I like. I think that I'm just getting the hang of what this is all about. So what are you going to visualize, Mike?"

"That's easy," Mike said with a smile. "I'll go fishing."

"Excellent, boys, excellent," Deliverance chuckled. "The whole point is that your place must be one that you are enthusiastic about, a place you want to visit. So, when you reach the bottom of the steps, I will cease to guide you any further. Gus will go to his coffee house in the plaza and create poetry. Mac will go trekking in the natural wilderness. Steve will go into his summerhouse and listen to soul music or read. And Mike will go fishing. It all sounds good. I will remain silent for around ten to fifteen minutes, then I will bring you out of it. Before I do that, I will say, *one minute*, so you can get ready."

"That's not long," Steve said.

"Actually, in a nonlinear reality, you will be surprised," Deliverance replied. "A metaphysical reality is not subject to physical time. Anyway, this exercise is simply to teach you how to do it. When you are alone, you can take as long as you like. Be aware, however, that more is not necessarily better. It is about quality of experience, not quantity.

"Right, backs straight, spines upright for flow. Close your eyes, gently and easily. Relax. Let the little muscles around the eyes relax. Let the tension out of your head, all the worries. Let them, and the stress they create, just drop away. Take the protective steel plate from the top of your head ... you are perfectly safe ... and imagine that the top of your head is a clear, still, tranquil pond ... let your jaw relax, and your throat ... and feel that wave of gentle relaxation creeping down to your solar plexus.

"Remove the subconscious psychic barrier that shields your solar plexus ... this is important ... and feel your solar plexus becoming soft, warm, open and vulnerable. Your arms, legs, your whole physical body is relaxing, becoming more and more relaxed, but as a Being of Light, you are awake and aware.

"Focus lovingly and respectfully on your physical body and identity. Feel good about yourself ... now visualize and imagine a body of Light that contains your physical body. This Light body is always with you, so you do not have to create it with your imagination. Just allow your imagination to find it, to see it, and to be aware of it.

"Now, release your identity focus and place your sense of self ... all that you think of as you ... in that Light body. You are now aware of self as a magnificent Being of Light. This, in fact, is your greater reality — Truth.

"Within your inner vision a rainbow appears, the colors a beautiful invitation. As a Being of Light, step away from your physical body ... you are safe ... and walking across to the rainbow ... step into the color red. As red flows through your lightness of Being, let it take away all remaining physical tension ... now step into orange. As orange flows through your lightness of Being, let it take away all anxiety and fears that you are ready to release ... move on into yellow. As yellow flows through your lightness of Being, let it take away all distracting, analysing, unwanted thoughts, leaving you clear, focused and open ... so you can enter green, where the peace of Nature enfolds and embraces you ... continue on into blue, the vibrant, healing energy of love ... and on into the spiritual upliftment of purple, raising you to a higher state of consciousness ... where you may enter and absorb the violet light of harmony.

"As you leave the rainbow, there is a large sphere of white Light before you. You enter the sphere, and walk slowly through it ... emerging as a Being of Light, vibrant, healed, and energized. Before you, there are twenty-one steps leading down to a greater Reality. These steps are illuminated by Light, very safe, and you know that you are ready. You go down the steps, beginning at 21, 20, 19, 18, 17, 16, 15, 14, 13, 12, 11 ... deeper ... deeper ... 10, 9, 8, 7, 6, 5, 4, 3, 2, 1.

"From the last step, you walk into your own, inner, creative reality."

CHAPTER TEN

AND IT ALL COMES TOGETHER

Ten minutes passed, then twelve, and Deliverance felt that they were ready to return. "One minute," he said. Another minute passed. "Come now, back to the steps ... it is time now to go back up the steps, beginning at 1, 2, 3, 4, 5, 6, 7, 8, 9, 10, 11, 12, 13, 14, 15, 16, 17, 18, 19, 20, 21. Leaving the steps, you walk across to the beautiful rainbow, entering into the color violet ... indigo ... blue ... green ... yellow ... orange ... and into red.

"Leaving the rainbow as a Being of Light, you walk back to your identity-body self. As you enfold and embrace your physical body in the Light of self, you are aware of the Light of self permeating and penetrating into every cell of your physical body. You realize that, just as your body is contained in the Light of self, so also each cell, every molecule, is contained in this radiant Light of self. It is your choice whether you live in the illumination of this Light or in the darkness of self-denial.

"You realize that, although you have a physical body, and that this body is yours, it is not who you are. You are a magnificent, metaphysical, Being of Light. This is your Truth. And, if you focus on and live this Truth, then Truth shall set you free.

"Now, switch your focus away from your Light-body self, back to your physical-identity self. Take a deep breath, filling your lungs ... and breathe out slowly. Once more, breathing in deeply, hold, and breathe out slowly. And one more time, breathe in deeply, hold, and as you breathe out slowly, you may open your eyes."

One by one, Mike and his friends opened their eyes.

"That was neat," Steve said approvingly. "I was able to follow it easier than I expected, but what really surprised me was the music I heard in the summer house. I put a CD in the player of some music that I like but have seldom listened to, and it played as clear as day." He looked at Deliverance with suspicion. "Did you put Tony O'Conner music on?"

Deliverance laughed and shook his head. "If I had, do you not think that we would all have heard it? Tell me, could you replace your thoughts of self-pity with a quick trip into the summerhouse?"

"Could I ever?" Steve laughed. "Any time."

"I thought that I'd find it easy," Gus mused, "but it wasn't. I had to really stay focused. My thoughts wanted to lead me astray and scatter me. Anyway, I did get into my favourite coffee shop, and amazingly, I was able to compose some poetry that I'm going to need to write down very soon."

Deliverance immediately went over to a small desk, returning with a writing pad and pen. "Be my guest, before you forget it," he said, offering them to Gus.

With a murmur of thanks, Gus retired to a far corner, his eyes screwed up with concentration.

"How did you go, Mac?" asked Mike.

"I surprised myself," Mac said smugly. "I thought it would be difficult. But when I left that last step, to my astonishment, I was in the wilds of Alaska, a place I've never visited but always wanted to. I was walking along a well-defined trail, and the ground was lightly covered with snow. That really surprised me. I got totally involved. It was great!"

"Did you have any sexual thoughts or feelings as you followed the trail?" Deliverance asked.

"No way. I seldom do when I'm absorbed in something I

enjoy," Mac replied.

"Let us be clear about this," Deliverance said. "What you have just experienced is reality. I told you earlier, reality is not all physical and linear; reality is also metaphysical and nonlinear. If you believe in nothing beyond a linear reality, then you will live half a life."

"Is that part of a consensus reality?" Mike asked.

Deliverance nodded. "Sadly, yes."

"So this wasn't a fantasy," Gus said.

"No. You were just touching on the edges of a greater reality," Deliverance replied. He looked at Mac. "To continue, do you think that when your everyday thoughts turn to sex, you can deliberately turn your thoughts toward your Light-body self and enjoy a bit of wilderness hiking instead? This way, instead of fighting unwanted thoughts and creating inner conflict, you simply redirect your focus."

Mac nodded decisively. "Yes, but it's a long time to be focused away from reality. That is, a physical reality," he rapidly corrected.

Deliverance chuckled. "You are getting the idea, son. And as for time, that is not a problem. Each time you do this inner exercise, you open up new synapses in the brain, new avenues for mental creativity to flow in and create. Quite quickly, you will learn to recognize the *feeling* of inner exercises. And, as quick as rapidly thinking your way through the opening process, you will be there, at the bottom of the steps. After a while, it is as though you hit a switch in your consciousness."

"Yeah," Mike said. "I experience it that way. My consciousness knows as soon as I close my eyes and focus. And then there is the feeling of spaciousness ... and difference. But I do remember, that when I began a few years ago, it was all resistance. My mind would chatter inane nonsense like a monkey. It didn't take long to get past that, but I guess Gus is going to have to go through that stage."

"Did I hear my name?" Gus asked, as he rejoined them.

"Yeah, it was me," Mike said, repeating it to Gus.

"Would you like to share your poetry?" Mac asked.

Gus looked embarrassed. "I don't think you guys want to hear my feeble poetry." He sighed, as he saw Deliverance gaze at him with gleaming eyes. "Okay, okay. My *brilliant* poetry is what I mean."

"Well if it's brilliant we all want to hear it," Steve said.

"Okay, I know when I'm beaten," Gus said. Then rapidly, "Cancel that. What I mean is, I know when it's time to concede that I must share my poetry with you."

Deliverance nodded, smiling. "It really is sinking in ... the power of the spoken word. We live our thoughts and our words, remember? So make sure they honor you. Right, Gus, over to you."

Gus took a deep breath and glanced at his paper. When he spoke, he looked them in the eyes.

"Deep within, beyond the ebbing tide of shallow despair,
there lies the vast and boundless depths of Self.
To simply dive, forever down, into the depths of Self,
and I shall know that all is new.
Forever new.
Beyond the ebbing tide.
I do not wait, but go to meet the boundless depths."

Silence met his words, lasting for long moments.

"Wow!" Steve exclaimed. "If that don't beat all. I didn't know that you had poetry like that in you, Gus."

"Nor did I," Gus said, wide-eyed. "Generally my poetry is mundane, cynical stuff."

"Now, that is what I call using inner energy very creatively," Deliverance stated. "I like it, Gus. Well done. Your words suggest that your wisdom is alive and well and longing to join with you in creating a life that will honor you. Go for it. I think you will find that the reason this poem lacks cynicism is because it came from a deeper aspect of your self. Touch into the magnificent Being that you are, and you will find no criticism, no cynicism, and no negativity. Just the heart of life."

"You often use the word *honor* in your conversation, and in a general sense I know what it means," Steve said. "But I get the feeling that, for you, honor is very important. When we first met ... my God ... just a few days ago, you said something about honor being the most important principle. Could you expand on this, please?"

Deliverance nodded. "I fully intend to talk about self-honoring when the moment arrives. And it is close! Realize, boys, that Truth shared in timing is Truth received. Out of timing, they are simply words that add up to something that the intellect thinks it knows. The intellect knows the sum meaning of the words, but it has no idea of the wisdom they contain. Wisdom is not the meaning of words; it is connecting with the essence of the contained experience. Wisdom is not a linear experience, it is a spherical experience. In other words, what you perceive as wisdom is held in a simultaneous moment that brings the past and the future into the now."

Deliverance chuckled. "To put it simply, wisdom is a heart event, not a head event!"

"I hope we'll get to talk about honor," Mike said, "but can we follow this a bit further? Are you saying that the heart experience is spatial, while the head experience is linear?"

"Yes. Well said. That is exactly what I am saying. The heart is about intelligence, while the head is about the intellect. Society today is brain/intellect driven, dominated by a science which predominantly has lost its heart/intelligence. You only have to look at our environment, our governments and our medical progress to see this. I am not saying that this is wrong or right. Simply, it is the way things are."

"But it is not the way that it has to be?" Steve asked.

"No, but it does reflect the mass human consciousness."

"So, what you are saying is that where we are at as a human species and what we are getting in our daily life is not the fault of a few, like the governments or the leaders in their various fields of endeavor?" Gus said. "It is people like me with similar problems and hang-ups, who run the countries and lead science and medicine, that are flawed in their thinking, in their whole view of life, and in their relationships with themselves and reality. Therefore, humanity reaps that effect. Is that it?"

"Unfortunately, yes," Deliverance nodded. "Today's heroes and heroines are not selected for their wisdom. Sport and business acumen are applauded, but how many people even want to know about Truth? It comes back to timing, boys. It has been said that humanity went to sleep *en masse*. Waking up is a one-by-one process. The key to awakening can only be turned in perfect personal timing. Until then, the door to a greater reality remains locked."

"Are we now turning that key?" Steve asked hopefully.

"Let us say you are approaching the door and aware of its reality," Deliverance said with a smile. "But be very sure you can unlock it and pass through. It is your choice. The only rule is: to enter, you are required to live the choice. Be happy that you now know that there is a door!"

Glancing at an antique grandfather clock loudly ticking in a corner, Deliverance looked to the others as he rose to his feet. "Come along, boys, back to the table and you can have your just desserts." He smiled at his own joke.

They followed him back into the dining room, which by now was emptying of patrons. After they each had chosen an extravagant and mouthwatering temptation, they sat back in their chairs, finishing their forgotten drinks.

"We will discuss honor another evening," Deliverance said. "I do not want to see you boys for another week. During that time, I want you to practice daily at what I have shown you. When your thoughts lead you toward places you do not want to revisit, take back your inherent power. Focus on an inner journey and do it as many times in the day as is required. You do not have to sit down and close your eyes. Just as your thoughts can run amuck while you are working, so they can be channelled into wonderful and uplifting avenues."

"I haven't told Harriet about you yet. The fact that I've been very late home for the last few nights intrigues her a bit, but worries her not at all," Gus said. "But should I tell her? Should I tell her that I am about to become a different person?"

"That choice is entirely yours," Deliverance said, "but I would suggest that you do not tell her. Live your Truth and let your newness shine through like a beacon. Live your Light so that all the old sameness is consumed in the illumination of your new way of being."

His eyes picked out Gus, Steve and Mac. "Listen to me very carefully. You will be under great pressure from the people in your lives to continue being the same individuals that you always have been. You will be pressured to conform. You will be expected to remain as you were. Am I being very clear? Do not fight that pressure, nor resist. What other people think and expect of you has nothing to do with you, nor can you control it.

"All your focus is on living and being the new you. If you tell people that you have changed, you invite ridicule. If you live a changed life, other people will say *you have changed*, and you can say, "Yes, I have. I now live a life that honors me." Never be afraid of your Truth, even if you get mocked for it. As soon as you even begin to leave consensus reality, the pressure will be on you. Dare to be who you really are. To be true to yourself does require courage, but it is a courage that we all have. Use it."

He looked at Gus. "This will be the most difficult for you. Mac and Steve basically live alone, and Mike is well along on this path, with a wife who is a supportive participant. But you will have a hostile wife and two puzzled daughters to deal with. So remember, it is all about focus. Do not attempt to lecture or to change them to accommodate you. Withdraw your emotional need from them, but give to them all the emotional support that you can. This is very important, but I will not explain it. When next we meet, you can tell me about it."

Holding them all with his magnetic eyes, he smiled. "We have not had many evenings together, but they have added up to a lot of hours that I have shared Truth with you. Now it is your turn. Truth must be lived. Do not fight anything in life, not even your sickness. Embrace it, learn from it, and then release it. Nothing ... I repeat, nothing comes into your life by accident. Another year, maybe, when I see that you boys are all ready, we will take this a lot deeper. For now, it is all ahead of you, and I know that you can do this."

"How do you know so definitely?" Gus asked

"Because I only spend time with people teaching and talking about the Principles of Truth when their timing has arrived," Deliverance said. "So if you are going to be challenged by this new way of living — and even that is your choice — then know that you can prevail."

Mike laughed softly. "I was listening to you so intently that I really didn't taste a thing of what I ate. What a waste!"

"Would you like some more?" Deliverance asked.

"Oh, no," Mike said, "I just thought it amusing."

"Well, you can be amused by me, too," Steve said. "I don't even remember eating mine, but it's gone."

Laughing, Gus and Mac nodded agreement.

"How about a week from tonight, boys? Can you manage that without any trouble?"

"I'm not sure about me," Mike said wistfully.

"We will discuss your situation later," Deliverance said.

"No problem for me," Steve said jauntily.

"Nor me," chimed in Gus and Mac.

The next morning, at Deliverance's invitation, Mike joined him in the garden alcove for a coffee. As always, Deliverance drank grapefruit juice. The atmosphere was a very relaxed, non-teaching mode.

"I take it you spoke with Tessa this morning as usual?" Deliverance asked.

Mike nodded. "Yeah. I phone her at her work place each morning at nine o'clock. She wants me to come home," he grinned. "As the old cliche says, absence makes the heart grow fonder. We have never been apart before, so at least it's shown us how much we enjoy each other's company and dislike being parted. I thought that I'd leave about lunch time. Then, with an overnight stop, I'll get home in good time tomorrow."

He sighed. "I'd love to stay and continue with this, but I also miss Tessa and the kids." He hesitated, unsure of himself. "Is there any chance that you could come and stay with us at some time in the future? Of course, only when it's convenient for you," he finished in a rush.

"Actually, I would be delighted to accept your invitation. But first, you must talk that over with Tessa. Who knows, it lies within the realms of possibility that we could all holiday in my beachside home next summer. We will see. Before you go, I will give you my e-mail address, and we can keep in touch."

Mike stared at him, his eyes shining in delight. "Oh, wow! We would both love that, take my word for it. Tessa is just as deeply into this new awareness as I am, and much more intuitive. She's just great."

"There is one thing that you may have forgotten," said Deliverance. "Before you go, it is time for you to receive the magic formula."

Mike stared at him. "My God! I had forgotten. I'm so keen to get back to Tessa it completely slipped my mind. But not only that, I feel that I've received so much already."

"I'm glad you feel that way," Deliverance smiled.

And he gave Mike a flat parcel, along with the magic formula.

A week passed.

CHAPTER ELEVEN

CHANGES ON THE WAY

When Gus, Mac and Steve walked into The Offbeat Eatery, it was ten minutes to eight. They went over to their usual table, set in a secluded position well away from the other diners, each feeling a bit of apprehension about what might be expected of him on a personal level.

Deliverance joined them almost before they were seated.

"Well, boys, it's nice to see you again." He looked them each searchingly in the eyes, and nodded. "One of you has had a hard time, while two have a fairly high and positive energy. However, before we start discussing your progress, we will get your dinner ordered."

Steve chose a simple fish and chips, while Mac and Gus each chose steak and salad. Drinks were quickly served, and Gus raised his glass. "How about a toast to an absent friend."

"Here's to Mike," Mac and Steve intoned, as they all tipped back their own particular drinks.

"So, Steve. Perhaps you could begin," Deliverance said.

Steve hesitated, a look of embarrassment on his face. "I'll tell you one thing," he said defiantly, "it ain't easy."

"Nobody suggested that it would be," Deliverance replied. "Although it is as easy or difficult as you choose."

"Yeah, I realize that, but the pressure from my buddies to remain the same was stronger than I expected. What really got to me was when I finally accepted that I had to make the choice of me changing without my buddies or remaining the same me with them. It didn't take long to see I couldn't have both."

"So what did you choose?" Mac asked.

"I chose me ... and change, but it wasn't easy. It took two or three days before they realized that I was serious. Then Dino, my best buddy, and I had a wing-ding row, and he walked out on me. That didn't feel so good. But the clincher came the next day, when he phoned me. He said that he was prepared to accept my apology and forget it. Then I blew up! Anyway, the outcome is, my buddies are out of my life, or to be more accurate, I'm out of theirs!"

Steve squinted his eyes thoughtfully. "It kinda hurt. We've been together for seven or eight years and shared some good times. But you know what's odd? I can't remember any! All I can remember is getting ever deeper into the shit, and Dino making it clear that this was the stuff of life. I ain't proud of the fact that I drifted along in Dino's wake like a little puppy dog. He and the others were all about six to ten years older than me, and I kinda thought that they knew where life was at. Especially Dino. He seemed so street wise. When he and I became best buddies, I was proud as hell. It felt like I had made the grade.

"Some grade!" He grinned sheepishly. "So, now that I'm divorced from my buddies, I'm on my own. And you know what? Once I got over the shock, it felt good. From now on, I paddle my own canoe. I think what really shocked me was their anger at me for wanting to change. They just couldn't understand it. I really expected that they would see how much better life would be for all of us. Man, was I wrong. I didn't let them go, they simply ditched me. It was almost as though they were ... scared ... or ... I don't know."

"Threatened?" Deliverance suggested.

"Yeah, that's it exactly," Steve exclaimed. "It's like they just couldn't handle either me or what I talked about. They told me to back off and get out of their faces." He sighed. "Well, although I had misgivings about them wanting to change, I decided that I'd give it the one shot." He smiled. "I obviously missed. Poor shot!"

"So how do you feel about it all now?" Gus asked. "Don't you have any regrets?"

"I feel good ... now. That took a few days. I guess I was surprised that they would dump me so quickly over such a small matter. But I've got no real regrets."

"Small matter!" Gus said, eyebrows raised.

"Yeah, well, maybe it ain't so small," Steve smiled. "When you come to think about it, that's a pretty dumb way to describe changing your life. Yeah, you're right. Small, it ain't."

"Tell me, how are you now?" Deliverance asked patiently.

"I'm good," Steve replied, nodding thoughtfully. "I didn't get into self-pity when they dumped me, and that's a change, for starters. I rationalized that it was inevitable, even though I'd tried to avoid facing it. When I felt an attack of *poor me* coming on, I made my way into the summerhouse, often two or three times a day. And I must say, even in only a week, I'm finding the inner exercise easier and more powerful. All in all, I've had a positive week, and ... now that I think about it, things have gone well for me. I decided not to move, and I've applied for two new jobs. And I now have an interview for one of them. That's progress. I haven't had a steady job for quite a while, and job interviews just didn't seem to happen."

"Any questions?" Deliverance asked.

Steve shook his head. "I had several the first day, but life seems to have taken care of things, and I like where I'm headed. To tell the truth, I'm getting to rather like me!"

Deliverance laughed and clapped his hands softly. "Now that is progress. Once you have established a good honoring relationship with yourself, you will find that life rewards you. Very good,

Steve, and congratulations."

As though his hand clap had been a summons, their dinner arrived, and for a few minutes eating was their main concern.

Deliverance sipped his grapefruit juice as he watched them affectionately. Finally, his eyes settled on Gus. "Are you ready to share your week's experiences with us?"

"I'm about as ready as I'll ever be," Gus replied. "To be honest, I didn't find it anywhere near as difficult as I expected it to be. But — and it's a big but — I did have to pay more attention to my moment-by-moment daily living than I have ever done. Generally, I just sort of drift through the day. Actually, no, that's not what I mean. I'll try again. Normally, each day is a repeat pattern of yesterday, and I'd follow that pattern in an incredibly unaware state. It's a bit like seeing a movie that you thought was new, but as you watch it, you get the feeling that you've seen it before. My life was like that. Notice I said ... was! For a week now, I've been really paying attention to me during my day. I've watched me react when I didn't even realize I was reacting. But I saw it, several times, and I decided that I could change it. Now, I'm reacting less and less to the old habitual stimuli. I'm taking command of my life. And this is just on one level, at work."

He smiled at the others. "Home life was something else again. I don't honestly believe anybody at work is the slightest bit aware of the effort that I'm making to change. Or even cares, for that matter. They all have their own crosses to bear. But at home! They keep asking me if I'm all right! I've been complimenting them, offering help, and generally being a nice guy. I've been doing what you suggested, Deliverance. I've been giving them emotional support in every way that I could, especially my girls. A week ago I would have said *the* girls, but already they feel like *my* girls once more. I discovered exactly what you knew that I'd discover. In supporting them, I have felt stronger. And in feeling stronger, so much of my former emotional need has melted away.

"I'm revelling in being the supporter instead of a wounded duck looking for, and needing, emotional support. I discovered — with a shock — that I don't have a fraction of the emotional need that I thought I did. It was a habit. A stupid, self-defeating habit that I carried with me from my childhood."

Gus straightened himself. "And another thing; I decided that I'm into this, full on. So, I've changed my diet. When I get home from work, I make myself a large salad, with only a small piece of meat, and no booze. Before, at the least, it was half a chicken with a tiny portion of cooked veggies, all washed down with a couple or three beers, and then a cigar. Man, if this is change, I'm into it! I'm aiming at losing fifty pounds in weight, and, by God, I'm going to do it."

"Good for you. Any comments from Harriet?" Mac asked.

Gus laughed. "I'm glad you asked. Harriet is the real clincher. Last night when we went to bed — and still in the same room and same bed would you believe — she asked me in a very concerned voice if I was feeling all right. And guess what I told her? I told her that I had recently discovered that I was dying. To my utter amazement, she began to cry. I was so shocked. Anyway, to cut a long story short, I explained that I was not dying of illness or cancer or anything like that, but that I was dying of sameness."

Gus grinned broadly. "She just couldn't understand what I was talking about, so without mentioning us, I told her some of the things I've learned from Deliverance. I told her that, with her or without her, my life would never be the same again. And I told her that I'm going to lose fifty pounds in weight. She laughed at first, but not much; and she mocked me a bit, but not much. She didn't react the way I'd expected. I thought that she'd be full of derision and scorn. But instead, she was ... sort of ... thoughtful."

"Why tell her about losing weight?" Steve asked. "Won't that put pressure on you?"

"Exactly right," Gus nodded emphatically. "And that's exactly what I want. I want everyone who knows me to know that I'm going to lose that weight. It means that I have to or look an absolute fool. And, believe me, I've finished with that. I don't mind telling you, when we first met Deliverance I was as sceptical as hell, but somewhere in it all, it suddenly clicked. I knew that this was it. Either I act on the wisdom of a living Master ... or I say an early good-bye to life. And deep down, in the boundless self, I knew that I could do it. As Deliverance says, *it's all about timing*, and my time has arrived."

He looked Deliverance in the eyes. "So that's my story. I've had a good week, really good. As for self-pity, I haven't had time. I've been too busy bringing Light into my life and into my family's lives. And that's what I intend to continue. What really leaves me astonished is the fact that my emotional dependency — which was so powerful that it was wrecking my life — was just a dream filled with shadows. All the power it had was fed to it by me. My emotional need had no power of its own. Once I changed my program, that formerly overpowering need was vanquished like a shadow in the Light. Now, day by day, I'm building a new life. I just know that my family is going to become a complete and happy unit again."

"And this is before we even get the formula," Steve joked.

Deliverance reached across the table and clasped Gus's hands. "I am so happy for you. This is what happens when the timing is correct. When Truth ignites life, life ignites with living Truth."

He turned to Mac. "It is your turn next, my friend, but you had better order your desserts first."

Plates were quickly whisked away, and their orders taken. Mac chose a macadamia ice cream, while Gus and Steve settled for fresh fruit. Sitting at the table with Deliverance had the advantage that their meals were delivered with brisk efficiency.

Steve and Gus both felt slightly uneasy, for they were aware by now that it was Mac who'd had the difficult week.

Mac was halfway through his ice cream before he looked up at the others.

"Well, it's obvious that I'm the problem here. I wish I could say that it's been as positive an experience for me as it was for Gus, but it hasn't. I've really struggled my way through this last week. I only hope that the magic formula is potent, because I sure do need a miracle."

"What was the main problem?" Deliverance asked.

"Depression and sexual fantasies," Mac said. "I tried all that you told us, or what I could remember, but I didn't get very far. First of all, my decision to quit work from highly paid to speculation and risk terrified me. Plain and simply, it frightened the shit out of me. I literally had diarrhoea! I was so anxious about the whole thing that I changed my decision back and forth until I was thoroughly depressed and miserable. Then the subconscious mind kicked in, offering sexual fantasies and false relief. God! What a mess! What a merry-go-round."

"Doesn't sound much like a merry-go-round to me," Steve said. "It sounds more like a misery-go-round. So what happened to the inner exercise? You know, trekking with your Light-body in Alaska. Surely that must have helped."

Mac groaned. "I just couldn't get the focus going. I'd shut my eyes, and by the time I was going down the steps, I was either asleep or my thoughts scattered every which way. All in all, my week has been worse than usual because now I feel that I should be able to do better. I feel that I have a way out, but I'm not using it, or not able to. I don't know which."

He looked at Deliverance pleadingly. "I do know that I need

help. Despite all that you've given me, it isn't enough."

"Deep down in your subconscious, you have become the complete victim," Deliverance said. "You victimize yourself. I expect you have noticed that nobody else is messing up your life. It's all your own work ... or is it? Tell me, what was your relationship like with your mother?"

There was a long silence while Mac stared miserably at the far wall, his face reflecting his inner conflict. Finally, he sighed, deep and shuddering. Taking a long, strangled breath, he looked at the others, noting the sympathy and concern in their eyes.

"I've never told anyone about this, but I think that finally I've got no choice. I can't go on like this. It all began when I was a kid. My mother ... beat me up ... when I was a boy. If she asked me to do anything, when I did it, it was either wrong or not good enough, and then she'd bash the living daylights out of me. Then, when I was crying and beaten, she would cuddle me and stroke my eyebrows. Later, as I got to be about ten or so, she would bash me, and then when she cuddled me, she'd stroke my cock and masturbate me. I ... got so ..." Mac stopped and began to quietly cry, his shoulders shaking as he tried to suppress it.

Moving to sit closer to him, Deliverance put an arm around Mac's shoulders and just held him. He said nothing, allowing Mac to grieve for his abused childhood.

Ten minutes passed in silence. Steve noticed that their table had been placed further away from the main dining area, more isolated than before, almost as though someone had known that this might happen. None of the other diners were aware of the unfolding drama at this particular table.

Taking a shuddering breath, Mac murmured his thanks to Deliverance. "I've got to finish this," he said quietly. "I got so sexually confused as I grew up that I didn't know whether I was repelled by women or attracted by them. Overall, I wanted a woman in my life, but I ... I ... I ... was impotent with a woman, responding only to masturbation." He sighed.

"I've been to various shrinks and therapists, and they helped some, but nothing that resolved my problem. You can see now, with all my self-loathing and self-disgust, why it was so important for me to be seen as a distinguished professor. I based my self-esteem in it. The only problem was, I came to hate the whole academic world of what I taught and the hypocrisy of my life."

Deliverance looked across the dining room, and holding his hand high, his forefinger and thumb making a circle, he loudly snapped the finger of his other hand. Within moments a waiter appeared, bearing a small drinks tray with a goblet of brandy.

"Drink this, son," Deliverance said as he put the glass of brandy into Mac's unresisting hand.

Mac sipped and coughed, his eyes watering, then sipped again. He nodded. "Thanks. That helps."

"Now that you have disgorged your unpalatable past to your friends and intimates," Deliverance continued, "the healing can begin. You have become truly vulnerable for the first time. Sharing with a therapist is not the same as sharing with your friends. The therapist has no past with you, and all is in confidence. But there are times when your need is to become vulnerable and exposed, the very thing that you most avoid happening. Having shared this secret that so shames you, I want you to look each of us in our eyes to see if you can see disgust, or loathing, or any form of rejection of you."

For long moments, Mac stared at the melted remains of his ice cream. Then, almost fearfully, he stared into Steve's eyes.

"No disgust or loathing here, old buddy," Steve said, "In fact, this is the first time I could ever say this to you, but I love you. I used to think that you were an arrogant, up-yours type of prick, but through these meetings I've learned that judgement based on what you think you see ain't such a good idea."

Mac smiled. "Thanks Steve."

He then looked into the eyes of Gus.

Gus leaned over the table, and reaching over to Mac, he slipped a hand over his neck and pulled him closer. "Look hard and long, Mac, and you'll see a buddy who really cares about you. Not only that, you can count on my help or support in any way that I can offer it, anytime."

He held onto Mac's neck, and despite the physical discomfort, Mac did not struggle. He knew that sincerity held him, and he enjoyed it.

When Gus let go, Mac sat back and rubbed his neck with a grin. "Thanks guys, I really appreciate it. You have no idea how it helps."

Shyly, he looked at Deliverance, and what he saw in those blue eyes held him. Nameless and formless, an energy wove its way into his very psyche, calming and reassuring him. Then, as suddenly as it started, it was gone.

"Did you see any disgust, or loathing, or any rejection?"

Mac shook his head mutely.

"Then give yourself the same care and consideration that your friends do. You have already learned about your past and its effect on you from your therapists, so you do not need to hear it repeated by me. But let me add this: anything of the past that is unresolved, is unresolved now. And it is in this now, this ongoing moment, that you can resolve it. First, as you well know, you are not to blame. And, strange as it may seem, neither is your mother. I can give you an almost ironclad guarantee that she was a victim of her own past and was most probably filled with horror and self-disgust by her own actions. A pattern you have repeated. That is the unfortunate way the negatives of life maintain and continue their existence. For as long as we look to blame, we empower and maintain blame. By taking responsibility for ourselves and our lives in each moment, we move out of, and beyond, the negative bonds of the past."

Looking into Mac's eyes, he asked, "Does this make sense to you?"

Mac nodded. "Yes, it does now, but a week ago it wouldn't. A week ago I would've said that you're crazy. Now, it all fits."

"I suggest that you put your decision to quit your academic career on hold," Deliverance said. "Take one step at a time. If you cannot jump a lake or a pond in a single leap, then begin by jumping puddles. Attempting to deal with everything in one go is just too much overload. So, begin with the depression and thoughts. You have been programmed into a cycle of guilt, so breaking out of this is your first objective. Who knows, when you really like yourself, you may well find that you like your job. Many people get confused in this area. They think that changing their work situations will change everything, but it does not. They take their program — their conditioning — with them. You have quite enough to deal with in breaking out of the cycle of guilt that began during your abusive childhood. And you have already begun to do this. You will find that, just by sharing it with us this evening, you have already lightened the burden.

"Do not try to establish a relationship with a woman at this time. As you have realized, there will be no salvation from a woman for you ... yet. You have to do this for yourself. For now, you need to establish an honoring relationship with yourself, and that will need all the attention that you can give it, and more. Later, who knows, a nurturing and supportive relationship with the right woman could be very fruitful, but everything needs to be developed and expressed in its perfect timing. First you grow the plant, and only then does it flower. This is the natural way to follow. A plant, be it bulb or whatever, cannot flower without the foundation of growth to store flower energy. We are the same, and now is the time for you to build the foundation of self-respect that can bring forth the time of inner flowering. Are you with me?"

Mac nodded decisively. "I certainly am."

"Do you think that you can do this?"

"Yes, I'm pretty sure that I can. I have to admit, just sharing my past with you guys and not being rejected is just so ... liberating. It feels good. I feel lighter, as though I've put down an old and filthy burden. It feels like I've washed myself clean."

"You have," Deliverance replied, "except that it was never a burden of filth. It was the weight of sadness. Your mother was an emotionally sick woman, her needs and expression twisted and distorted as she victimized both you and her. The tragedy is that we inadvertently use wrong focus and continue the abuse. However, at this stage of rebuilding your life, you must take one issue at a time, and your mother is not the issue, you are. I understand that your mother is no longer alive?"

"No, she died years ago, of alcoholism."

"Now is the time to release her, if you have not already done so," Deliverance said.

"I thought I had," Mac replied, "but I see now that she sort of lives in my subconscious mind. When I masturbate, my self-disgust comes from the past, the same as I felt when she did it to me. I hated it because I liked it so much. It was that, more than anything, that set up the guilt. God! Talk about confusing. But I feel a definite response to what you said about the weight of my sadness. I can see now that sadness has been my companion for a long time, and I'm ready to let it go. And what you said about putting my decision to quit my job on hold feels good. You're right, it was all too much in one go. And you just may be right about work. I can remember when I really enjoyed my teaching work. I'm too confused and overloaded right now to work out where hating my work came from, but it could be a projection of hating myself seeping into hating what I do."

Mac looked at each of the others, a little smile on his lips.

"I really believe that I can do this now. I think that I'm at the place Gus described as 'pieces clicking into place.' I hadn't felt that before."

Deliverance glanced at his watch. "It's late, boys. I want you to practice for another two weeks, and then we meet here two weeks from tonight, on time."

He looked at Mac. "Use your inner exercise often to curb — not control — the mind. You will find that you can do it now without any difficulty. Tonight, you removed the blocks."

CHAPTER TWELVE

THE FINAL DELIVERY

When Mac, Steve and Gus strolled into The Offbeat Eatery two weeks later, they had an obvious bond between them that far exceeded their friendship of the past.

Deliverance was sitting at their table, waiting, a big smile on his face. A magnum of champagne stood in the center of the table, while three flat parcels lay close by.

"Welcome, boys, and take a seat. I have taken the liberty of ordering dinner for tonight, and it's on its way right now."

The waiter arrived, bearing small platters of oysters Kilpatrick. With big grins all round, and under the scrutiny of a smiling Deliverance, they tucked in.

"Mmmm," Steve said, "this is just about my favourite food."

"I'll make an exception tonight," Gus said, "because this has the feel of graduation night. But the new me has put this in the 'very occasional' category."

"If it's graduation night," Mac declared, "I'm ready. I've had a great couple of weeks, even if the first week was rather challenging. He speared a dripping oyster and held it high. Just like this oyster, I've come out of my shell. And like this oyster, I needed help." He looked at Deliverance with a cocky grin. "You delivered, Deliverance. From my heart, thank you."

Deliverance inclined his head gracefully. "My pleasure. It gives me a thrill that boys like you can turn your lives around by living your Truth. By doing so, others will follow your example, and in ever-increasing volume the ripples of harmony will softly caress the disturbed shores of other people's lives."

Their platters quickly emptied, the waiter cleared the table. Steve's eyes popped when a waitress came bearing a whole large baked salmon laid out on a silver tray. Steamed vegetables were served, and a tureen of shrimp sauce awaited those who cared to use it.

"Man!" Steve said happily. "You sure are some teacher, Deliverance. You not only feed the psyche and soul, but also the stomach. Wow! What a meal. I thank you, sir."

Waiting until they all were happily engaged in eating, and with their first hunger satisfied, Deliverance spoke to them.

"If you remember, boys, the first time we met I talked to you about the Principles of Truth. Throughout our following discussions, I have gradually introduced these Truths. I have told you also that to receive any benefits from these principles, they must be lived. Be very clear about that; Truth must be lived to become empowered and actualized. Truth, as words of knowledge only, is conceptual, empty and powerless. I repeat, you must live Truth to know Truth. Truth is an experience.

"You will, no doubt, remember that I told you the greatest of these principles is honor — to honor yourself. Now, listen carefully, boys, for I am going to give you a great Truth: *If you honor yourself, you honor life, and if you honor life, life will honor you.* There are many levels of meaning to these few simple words, but you only see into them at the depth that you are able. If you live this way, by honoring self, then the depths will, in perfect timing, reveal far greater insights.

"Later, in about another year, when you are the living embodiment of all that you have been learning, we will all get together again and take this deeper." His lips twitched in an ambiguous smile. "Maybe I will teach you about chickens and eagles and how to fly! I suggested to Mike that next year we all meet for a week in my beachside holiday home, and this includes those of your families who care to be involved."

"That would be wonderful. The way things are shaping up, not only will my girls be there, but Harriet, too," Gus said with enthusiasm. "You can't believe the difference this has made in my life. I've already lost seven pounds in weight, and I'm really enjoying the way I eat. Eating heaps of fresh fruit and vegetables gives me an inner vitality that I haven't felt since I was a kid. The family has stopped asking me if I'm all right, and they now treat me with respect. Respect! I hadn't felt respected as a person for years, apart from my work skills. Now, even better, I respect myself. And, would you believe, Harriet is asking for my advice and opinion in matters that she hasn't asked for in years."

"That's wonderful, Gus" Deliverance smiled.

"Yeah, that's great. You deserve it," Steve said. "I'm going great too, but I find that I need to go into my summer-house several times a day. Whenever self-pity or being the victim comes creeping in, away I go. And I'm definitely breaking the cycle. I saw Dino the other day down in our local coffee shop, and he grinned at me but made no move to talk. And I felt okay with that. I had nothing to say to him, anyway. But you haven't heard the really good news ... I've got a job. And, even better, I love it. I'm working in a Maritime museum, would you believe, so my old navy experience and my interest in nautical artifacts are now assets."

Steve grinned at them. "And so long as I know the date of that proposed holiday with you, Deliverance, nothing can keep me away. Again, sir, I thank you."

All eyes turned to Mac.

He sighed, a shy smile on his lips. "I'm still the lame duck here but ... !" He clapped a hand over his mouth, quickly forestalling Deliverance by rapidly announcing, "I was the lame duck here, but I'm now becoming a swan in my endeavors to honor myself. First of all, I have to say that releasing the decision to quit my job has taken a lot of the pressure off me. I'm going to give myself time with my present job. And if in another six months or so I really want to quit, then I'll be ready. The idea of being a wilderness tour guide certainly touches my heart, but I may be physically past it. Who knows? Meanwhile, the pressure's off me. I know that some people can take far more pressure than others, and I thought that I was one of them. But I've learned that I'm not. I have to face the fact that I don't thrive when I'm under pressure. And, silly as it may sound, knowing this really helps."

"There is nothing silly about that," Deliverance said. "We each have a different past and different abilities, and knowing your own capabilities is a part of wise living. Wisdom is the art of knowing your limits, but not allowing them to limit you." He smiled. "This may sound like a contradiction, but given time you will see beyond the surface of the words."

Mac nodded. "I don't understand that, yet, but I feel it. Anyway, back to my couple of weeks. I'm quite sure that dirty thoughts are an addiction. Seriously, as soon as my mind isn't occupied elsewhere, it starts to create sexual fantasies. It really aggravates me. Instead of me thinking thoughts, it seems that thoughts are thinking me! Anyway, every time my thoughts went in that direction, I set off through the rainbow and down the steps. My God! I've been to Alaska a lot of times in this past two weeks. And it does work. The trick is to go with something that really holds your interest and attention."

"You follow your heart," said Deliverance.

"Yeah, that's where it's at. And I really do love the trekking thing. I can see already, that given time, my mind and thoughts will be trained to move in a more creative and freeing direction. I have to be honest, I think that it'll take months, maybe even a few years, but I know that if I persist — and I will — I'll be the winner.

"What really gets to me is the thought that I could come back and repeat the same format for another lifetime. I'd rather bite the bullet and deal with it now. Break the cycle. So, all in all, I've struggled a bit, and that's okay. I realize now that it's okay to struggle so long as I persist. I get the feeling that tonight is the night we get to learn the magic formula, and I have to admit, it's only now that the timing is right for me. I got really pissed off with you for offering it but not telling us. I wanted a formula that could do this for me, but I've reached the place where I realize that this was just wishful thinking, a cop-out. No formula can change anything that we're not ready to take responsibility for, and I've only just reached that place. So, thanks, Deliverance, for making me wait. I'm going to be okay. I'm a winner."

Deliverance smiled warmly. "I am so glad you came to that particular insight by yourself. Mike was ready for the formula from the first day because he would not have made it his security, but you boys, one by one, have reached the place of taking responsibility for your own life.

"Hear me well. There is nothing more honoring in your life than to take responsibility for yourself and your life. When you detach yourself from all blaming and all faulting, knowing that it is you who writes the movie of your life, then you become a scriptwriter of newness instead of writing more of the same. As I have said, in another year we can take this into the larger picture of life, but Truth has its timing and Truth has its living. The living of Truth always precedes the time of Truth, and by doing so, creates the timing. Lived and experienced, they create a spiral of connectedness where the living and the timing are recognized as One. And you know that they were never separate.

"In your daily living, think thoughts that honor you. Think of yourself as worthy and deserving — and life delivers! Think of yourself as unworthy and non-deserving — and life withholds. And be aware of what you think. The deeply programmed, subconscious thoughts are the ones that run your life. They are the thoughts that you are not aware of thinking! This is the unaware living of the masses. Listen to your thoughts without criticism of them. Create deliberate thoughts of self-appreciation, self-acceptance and self-respect."

Deliverance looked at them each in turn. "I am proud of you boys. You have come a long way in quite a short time. So now, finally, it is time to give you the magic formula. You have proved yourselves worthy of receiving it."

Reaching to the flat parcels before him, he gave one to Gus, one to Steve, and one to Mac. He watched with an affectionate smile as they, hesitatingly, opened their parcels. Finally, they each held a medium-sized wall mirror and a small silk cloth of varying colors.

They looked at Deliverance with puzzled smiles.

"You will notice that each mirror is different. Gus, your mirror has a few memorable lines from the great poets inscribed in the brass surround. Mac, your mirror has scenes from the wilderness carved into the wood, while yours, Steve, has the musical notes of famous uplifting melodies inscribed in its silver surround. These mirrors have been personalized for each of you. You will also notice that the glass of each mirror has been sprayed with a swirl of rainbow colors so that there is no facial reflection except for your eyes. With no face or features, there is no judgement or bias. I want each of you to hang your mirror on the wall when you get home and place over it the small silk cloth so that other people cannot look into it. Mac, hold up your mirror cloth."

Mac did as he was asked, and they saw the words *Reflect*

and *Choose* printed over the background of a color-filled rainbow.

"Your mirror is personal to you, and you alone. Each morning I want you to lift the cloth from the mirror and look into your own eyes. And each morning I want you to consciously choose what you will be that day. Will I be an eagle or a chicken? Will I be magnificent or mundane? Will I live this day on a spiral or a cycle? Will it be a day of honoring myself or denying myself? Is it going to be a day of newness within myself and life or more of the past sameness? Will I live in the Light or play in the shadows? These are your choices to make, and when they are made, you cover the mirror and go and live your choices.

"At the end of the day, before you go to bed, you look into the eyes in the mirror and ask: was I an eagle today or a chicken? Was I magnificent or mundane? Did I live my day on the spiral or the cycle? Did I honor myself today or deny? Was my day new or was it more of the same? Did I live in the Light or was I lost in the shadows?

"When you have done this, there must be no judgement of yourself. You will find it far more difficult to judge your eyes than your whole facial reflection. By looking deep into your eyes, you will find that you are looking into your soul. It will lift this process onto a higher level. It will feel as though you are brand new, instead of the same, everyday face of the person whom you long ago judged as 'found wanting.' Looking into your eyes, you simply acknowledge how you lived that day and resolve, that because the next day is new and that you also are new, then newness will always be your choice. You can, with patience and attention, live each day as an eagle, magnificently spiralling into the Light of Newness in a way that honors you and honors life. Or, you can live as a chicken, on the mundane cycle of sameness, lost in the shadows, denying your potential.

"You must do this each day without fail; and, of course, each day you will choose to honor your Self. But each evening when you look in the mirror, you will learn that the path of honor does not just happen. It is a path that has to be walked with awareness, with attention, and with a great deal of patience. Do this, persist. As you gradually soar into the flight path of the eagle, so the greater view of life will be revealed."

"So that's the magic formula," Steve said. "Gee, I wondered what it would be. It all sounds pretty simple."

"Not to me, it doesn't," Mac said. "To me, it says that it's by my own efforts I either fly high like the eagle or shuffle around in the dirt like a chicken. Let's face it. Right now, I'm a chicken, but I want and intend to be an eagle. That I know."

"That's where we part company, pal," Gus said. "I'm starting on the premise that I'm an eagle, and I'm simply going to fly a whole lot higher. But, simple as it sounds, the formula is definitely confronting. Eyes only or not, I have to face me in that mirror, twice a day, and confront myself. For a guy who could use a mirror each day for shaving and manage not to really see myself, it's definitely a challenge. That's why I choose to start off by being the eagle. Who wants to see bloody chicken eyes staring back?"

"Tell me honestly, Deliverance, will it work?" Steve asked. "I mean, it doesn't sound very magic to me."

"Of course there is no magic in the formula, Steve," Deliverance replied, "but there is magic in you. Powerful magic. Each human Being has a potential that is far more powerful than magic and more potent than you could ever imagine. Trust me. You use that mirror in the way that I have told you, every day, and it will bring the magic of Self into your daily life. You see, unlike any other creatures on this planet, human beings have the ability to transform themselves. You can transform your self, your life and your universe. This is power. By using the mirror and applying the formula, magic which is so natural that it is eternally denied will enter your life. And beyond all questions and doubts, you will know it."

Standing up, Deliverance smiled at them fondly. "Of course, the day will come when you can clean off the mirror — it comes off very easily — and reveal your full face. You may want to do that a bit at a time, or all in one go. That's your choice, but taking my advice, don't rush it. It's your soul I want you to connect with, and your eyes are the entrance. When you feel revitalized and renewed to a soul level, and you know that it is permanent and that you are living in a new way, then it's time to expose the face and congratulate yourself.

So, boys, the next year is up to you. I have given you enough to begin that transformation, but only you can do it. If everything works out, sometime about a year from now we will have that time together in my coastal holiday home. Then, we can talk of other things."

Reaching for the magnum of champagne, he popped the cork, pouring the foaming liquid into the waiting glasses.

"A toast, my friends, to your new flight paths."

"To eagles," Steve said.

"To flying high," Mac and Gus said together, their glasses and heads held high.

Deliverance hugged them, one by one. "Until we meet again, boys, just remember: live your life from your heart, and you will never regret it. Remember what I said about honor, and live it. This is a great and powerful principle on which to base your life. If you honor yourself, you honor life, and if you honor life, life will honor you."

THE END

INFORMATION ON MICHAEL J. ROADS AND THE 5-DAY ROADSWAY RE*TREATS, AND SEMINARS

Michael Roads was born in 1937, in England. From his earliest years Michael delved into the mysteries of a hidden, silent nature. By young adulthood he had become an outdoorsman, farmer and gardener.

At 21 he married Treenie – "the smartest thing I ever did!" In their mid-twenties they emigrated with their two sons to Tasmania, the island state of Australia, where they continued farming for the next decade.

With a newly born desire for personal growth, feelings shared equally by Treenie, they sold their farm and embarked on a year's journey around Australia with their children, now numbering four. The culmination of their odyssey was the founding of an intentional community based on the Findhorn Foundation in Scotland. This was a time of challenge, inner growth and dynamic change. This also was the period during which Michael connected with the inner, metaphysical expression of nature.

Four years later they left the community to continue in their own way. In 1986 Michael went through a profound transformation of consciousness. The Truth of Life – life beyond body/mind/ego identity – was revealed to him with stunning clarity. Moving into this ever-expanding state of self-realization, he became the expression and experience of Truth.

*The wisdom unveiled in this conscious state of 'connection and insight' is the basis for Michael's books, currently in thirteen languages, and international seminars and Re*treats. Michael beautifully describes his transformation as, "Falling in love with Self."*

*Michael's and Treenie's speaking and Roadsway Re*treat tours have included invitations to Australia, New Zealand, South Africa, Holland, Italy, Switzerland, Austria, Belgium, Germany, UK, Denmark, West Indies, U.S.A., Canada and Japan. An extraordinarily gifted communicator, Michael imparts Truth heart-to-heart, far beyond the reach of words, creating the space to awaken from a dream ... to ignite the Truth alive within each person.*

He is the author of the BEYOND WORLDS *quartet;* TALKING WITH NATURE, JOURNEY INTO NATURE, JOURNEY INTO ONENESS *and* INTO A TIMELESS REALM. *He also is the author of the acclaimed U.S.A. 1999, 'Best Visionary Fiction of the Year,'* GETTING THERE.

*The Roadsway Re*treats are designed to provide a foundation for spiritual growth based on the self-empowering Principles of Truth.*

Michael and Treenie may be contacted for information about their annual tours, books, CD's, etc., at www.michaelroads.com. E-mail: roadsway@optusnet.com.au

For additional information on Michael's work as an author and contemporary teacher, including audio recordings, seminar/Re*treat schedules, and the ***Roadsway Newsletter***, or for information on sponsoring a weekend seminar for your group or organization, please contact:

The Roadsway

3029 Prospect Avenue
Cleveland, Ohio 44115
USA
216.588.0099
Fax: 216.391.1636
email: *roadsway@nacs.net*

Complimentary newsletter sent on request.